William Cullen / Doris Lehniger

B for Business

Instructor's Guide

A Complete English Course for Students of Business Studies

MAX HUEBER VERLAG

4. 3. 2. | Die letzten Ziffern
2008 07 06 05 04 | bezeichnen Zahl und Jahr des Druckes.
Alle Drucke dieser Auflage können, da unverändert, nebeneinander benutzt werden.
1. Auflage

Satz/Layout/Umschlaggestaltung: grafik & design, Bettina Kammerer, München
Druck und Bindung: Ludwig Auer GmbH, Donauwörth
Printed in Germany
ISBN 3-19-012702-6

CONTENTS

B FOR BUSINESS INSTRUCTOR'S GUIDE

Our mission in writing B for Business was:
- to provide students with a real-world book
- to present the best mix of traditional approaches and newer perspectives
- to give a foundation in the vocabulary, concepts and skills for a successful career in business

We hope that you enjoy our book.

INTRODUCTION

The material in this course book has been tested in co-operation with selected trainers in various course programmes and with advice from entrepreneurs, managers and communication consultants working in the domestic and international business environment. Testing of the material has clearly shown that students' communications skills have been substantially improved via the new terminology learned and from practice through the simulations and other activities.

TARGET GROUP

B for Business is a course material designed for participants in Business English courses at universities and other tertiary institutions including Berufsakademien and Wirtschaftsakademien who intend to pursue a career in business or are already in business-oriented work. We should emphasise that unlike other course books this material has been especially created to cater for those who do not have previous experience of the business world. Learners with experience will, however, profit from this approach.

The book contains sufficient material for about 100-150 hours of both class work and homework. This allows for a very flexible approach depending on the level and priorities of the learners and the degree of self-study. The material has been developed for students with an intermediate level of English and above. B for Business has been used successfully as UNIcert® Levels 2 and 3 preparation material. It is also suitable for this purpose for the

- London Chamber of Commerce and Industry (LCCI) Examinations
- University of Cambridge Local Examinations Syndicate (Business English Certificate Levels 2 and 3)
- Test of English for International Communication (TOEIC).

A SHORT NOTE ON UNICERT®

UNIcert® is a system of accreditation and certification agreed by a large and increasing number of universities in Germany and piloted by CercleS, the European Confederation of Language Centres in Higher Education. It aims to standardise the grades awarded by universities for various levels of modern language competence, to promote a greater degree of comparability between university language course programmes and thus to introduce a certificate which is valid and acceptable also beyond the university context, as an indication of practical foreign language ability as required by academically trained personnel. For more detailed information please visit the UNIcert® home page (http://rcswww.urz.tu-dresden.de/~unicert).

RATIONALE

The units of this topic- and skills-based course material are designed to be as close to reality as possible based on the real-life story of Hazel Browne and her attempts to set up a new business after completing her education. Hazel is busy both attending a young entrepreneurs' course and getting her new business off the ground.

The steps she undertakes provide the business background and vocabulary input needed for the students
- to communicate effectively in a business environment
- to read and analyse pertinent business materials
- to discuss relevant economic and business issues.

In addition, the material prepares course participants for a study period in English-speaking countries.

STRUCTURE

B for Business consists of a compact course book with two audio cassettes/CDs and an Instructor's Guide. The 15 units of the course book consist of a story line which provides a combination of reading, listening, speaking and writing practices. The appendix contains a grammar section and an extensive reference section.

Main Features:
- high degree of flexibility; although there is a clear progressing story line, the units can be used independently
- focus on oral communication
- high degree of student involvement through the use of role-plays and simulation activities which also foster the development of interpersonal skills
- extensive vocabulary list with translations, English language explanations and/or sample phrases
- links to relevant Internet addresses to develop learner autonomy (www.hueber.de)
- Grammar Section focussing on main areas of English grammar
- extensive Reference Section with detailed overview of language functions and skills such as presentations, telephoning, negotiating and social English
- concise Instructor's Guide with photocopiable material.

Vocabulary
The vocabulary in the book is intended for productive use. It should be pointed out that many of the words are not always in strict alphabetical order but often consist of connected word groups/collocations to help students to communicate on a certain topic. The vocabulary lists should be studied at home by the students before the commencement of each unit.

Listening
The listening comprehension exercises (phone calls, presentations, meetings, etc) are available on cassette or CD. They are part of the story line and an integral part of each unit.

Students at this level should understand that reading and listening at the same time does not help them to improve their listening comprehension. This approach should therefore be strictly avoided. It is important that instructors explain this clearly to their audience.

The guiding principle is that students should listen to the text the appropriate number of times, then attempt to do the exercises connected with it and only afterwards read the transcript for consolidation. Students might be reminded that when they are in English-speaking countries there is no transcript!

Writing
The book provides comprehensive insight into writing including standard types of commercial correspondence, e-mail and an introduction to reports as well as pertinent practice exercises. Other areas covered are note-taking (which is particularly important for learners who intend to spend a study period abroad), minutes of meetings, letters of application and a CV/Resumé.

Reading
The story-line approach offers students a wide variety of material and text types that are relevant in the day-to-day business world as well as accessible introductions to business concepts and terminology.

Simulation
The simulations give the students an opportunity to use the language they have learned from the course material in an imaginary real-life situation. Each simulation activity follows the steps of the story line.

The simulations can be done either unit by unit or as a separate concentrated module after completion of the book. They are group projects for which students should be divided into groups of six as a maximum, otherwise the opportunity to speak is reduced. The team works together on the respective task and finally presents the results to the whole class. Each group can be advised to do some of the preparation work for the simulations via e-mail. The simulation is also useful for revision.

The instructor should try to integrate different skills and insist that students use English. He/She should make sure that they understand the purpose of simulation activities, i.e. to develop their communicative competence in the foreign language.

Students should be advised to use a dictionary for unknown vocabulary. Instructors should supervise and assist them but interfere as little as possible. It is also important to evaluate the simulations at the end together with the students including extensive feedback on common errors.

Suggested Approach:
In the 1st session the students get approximately 45 minutes to brainstorm ideas for the respective simulation, to outline the necessary steps and discuss responsibilities. Then group members work out their (individual) parts in class or at home.

In the 2nd session the students work in groups for circa 30-45 minutes discussing and fine-tuning material and preparing for group presentation. Afterwards the group members present their project. All group members should be involved in the oral presentation. If time is pressing each group member should only be allotted 2-3 minutes for presenting his/her part. In any event the simulation should be completed by the end of the 3rd session. The last step should always be an evaluation of the simulation.

Grammar Section
A brief revision of grammar rules and accompanying exercises is included in a separate section. For more intensive revision students should be advised to refer to standard English grammar books (e.g. R. Murphy, *English Grammar in Use. New Edition.* Cambridge: CUP, 1994).

Reference Section
The extensive Reference Section has been devised to equip learners with a wide range of functions and skills to enhance their writing, reading, listening and speaking abilities. Throughout the units they are actively encouraged to refer to this section.

Internet Links
B for Business offers a home page with Internet links for each unit (www.hueber.de). Instructors should encourage students to use these links and/or surf the Internet for additional material relating to the respective topics.

Illustrations
Illustrations introduce the topic of each unit and can be used as the starting point for a lead-in discussion.

Story Line

Hazel Browne, the main character of the book, has just graduated and to decide her next step in life (see illustration, p. 5).

The unit starts with Hazel's CV and continues with a talk between her and the two authors, Doris and William, who are told about her plans to set up a firm manufacturing Celtic jewellery. Doris has recommended her to take part in a young entrepreneurs' course offered by the Jobcentre in order to prepare herself on how to run a business properly.

At the Jobcentre John Brennan, an official representing a stereotype Irish civil servant, informs her about the course. She signs up for it and is requested to hand in a business plan within the next few weeks. The following units will describe the ongoing process of Hazel attending the Young Entrepreneurs' course while simultaneously starting up her business.

Focus

- To enable students to talk about their education, student life and career
- To develop students' listening comprehension skills
- To introduce CV writing skills

Lead-in

Teachers should point out the fact that Hazel is Irish and the book has an Irish setting. This affords instructors the opportunity of introducing Ireland and comparing it with their own country, or with other English-speaking countries.

For detailed information about Ireland please refer to the Internet links for Unit 1 (www.hueber.de). Alternatively consult Gearóid Ó Chuláinn's *Ireland A–Z* (Cornelsen & Oxford, 1997) for a quick yet informative insight into all aspects of Irish life.

Students can also engage in a brainstorming session on Ireland. Those who have visited the country can recount their experiences and take questions from the class.

Another option is for the instructor to ask students to give short presentations on Irish economy, culture, history and current political situation.

6 CURRICULUM VITAE

Take students through CV. Explain that CV is British English while Resumé is American English and has another format (see p. 133). As there are many different styles in writing a CV Hazel's serves as an example. For more detailed information make sure students refer to Reference Section, p. 270.

▶ Note: The plural of *curriculum vitae* is *curricula vitae.*

Hazel's e-mail address hbrowne@kps.imw.ok-dublin.ie is read as follows: *hbrowne – one word – lower case lettering* (i.e. small letters as opposed to upper case lettering or capital letters) *at – k – p – s – dot – i – m – w – dot – o – k – dash – dublin – dot – i – e*

U.K. A-Levels, Irish School Leaving Certificate, North American High School Diploma and German *Abitur* are similar in standard.

A full driving licence is the standard in Continental Europe. However, in Ireland and the UK, a provisional licence can be issued before the driving test. A driver with a full licence must be present in the car and 'L' (Learner) signs must be visible both in the front and rear window.

1. The students discuss characteristic features of a CV. Sample answers could be: divided into categories, short and concise, chronological order, etc.
   Then the students compare Hazel's CV with what is standard in their own country and pay attention to differences in application procedures. For example, in English-speaking countries you would initially only send a CV/Resumé with a covering letter when applying for a job. Later originals or certified copies of most relevant certificates and references may be required by the prospective employer. CVs don't include a photograph.

7 – 9 FROM STUDENT TO ENTREPRENEUR

Students read or listen to the introductory paragraph, p. 7, and are encouraged to use the Internet links on the Hueber home page for supplementary information and consolidation. Afterwards, with books closed, they listen to the task given and the conversation between Hazel and the authors. Play the conversation twice if necessary and check for understanding. At this stage it should be pointed out to the students that reading and listening at the same time does not help learners to improve their listening comprehension. Remember to tell them that there is no script when they do a listening comprehension test or meet other English speakers in real-life situations.

This section may be a bit long for weaker groups. We suggest you break the listening up as follows:
1st part: Before Hazel started university. Stop cassette/CD at ... *was lucky enough to be accepted* (p.7).
2nd part: Hazel's life as a student. Stop cassette/CD at ... *she'll be eligible for the pension* (p. 9).
3rd part: Hazel's career path. Play to end.

Referring to task on p. 7 check comprehension.

▶ Note: The word *guy* is American and Australian English and refers to a male. The plural form *guys* is used to address a group of people whether they are male or female. Trinity College Dublin (TCD) is one of the oldest universities in the world and was opened by Queen Elizabeth I in 1592. It has exchange relations with British and American universities such as Oxford, Cambridge, Harvard and Yale. The photograph (p. 9) shows part of the Trinity College Dublin campus.

Now that you already know something about Hazel... 7

•What new things do you learn about Hazel?
She found the change from second level to third level really difficult.
Hazel did well in her studies and spent her first term at the student halls of residence.
Her roommate was Lisa.
Later she moved into her gran's flat.
She couldn't make the early morning lectures.
Hazel had around 30 hours a week at the university.
She had applied for some jobs without putting a lot of energy into it.
She doesn't like the 9-5 lifestyle.
The grasshead business was important for her to finance her "exotic lifestyle".
She wants to set up her own business (Celtic jewellery).
She's planning to take part in a Young Entrepreneurs' course to learn how to run a business properly.

• What did she like and dislike about being a student?
Hazel enjoyed her time as a student, liked learning languages, especially Spanish, the students' balls and discos, parties, the feeling of not being alone.
She disliked boring lectures, the feeling of anonymity in the lecture halls, too much theory, examination time, the early morning lectures, the lack of privacy in the halls of residence.

10 **Discussion**

Do relevant discussion.

2. For the description of their educational institute students University or college brochures/home pages can be used. As a preparation students should also refer to the relevant links to Trinity College Dublin and Kent State University.

Exercises

7. Translation exercise
   a) I took my A-levels in Berlin three years ago.
   b) After I had passed my final exams I applied for a place at Dresden University of Technology.
   c) Before I started my studies I did my military/civilian service.
   d) As my parents' income exceeds a certain limit I do not receive a student loan/grant (*Bafög* is a combination of the two).
   e) I have been studying at this university since October … and hope to graduate in the year … .
   f) After my basic studies I would like to apply for a practical training period/placement/internship abroad.
   g) The majority of the courses in the basic studies is/are compulsory and has/have to be attended by all students.
   h) The first academic degree at most British universities/colleges of further education is the Bachelor which is awarded/conferred after three years.
   i) The university/college offers accommodation in student hostels/halls of residence/dormitories, most of which are situated near/close to the campus.

If Nos 9 and 10 are to be attempted make sure the Reference Section is referred to. Alternatively, wait for similar exercises in Unit 8.

THE YOUNG ENTREPRENEURS' SCHEME 11

▶ Note: The photograph shows a UK jobcentre. A jobcentre in Ireland is referred to as a FÁS (Foras Áiseanna Saothair – the Training and Employment Authority) centre. Ireland has two official languages; Irish (Gaelic) and English.

The students open the book (p. 13) and answer the comprehension questions. Let them listen twice and check their answers.

Comprehension 13

1. To encourage more people to set up their own businesses, which is vital for the economy and export figures.
2. It is for people who are unemployed, have some experience in business, intend to set up their own venture and give the impression that they are able to succeed.
3. Yes, she does, as she is currently unemployed and was involved in running a business.
4. The applicant has to fill in an application form, may be called for an interview, may have to provide references, has to hand in a business plan.
5. The next course begins on 22 April.
6. The government is spending a lot of money on the Young Entrepreneurs' Scheme and, therefore, it expects serious candidates. The business plan shows whether the candidate has a clear idea of his/her project and will also help the prospective entrepreneur to focus on it.
7. The deadline is 5 June.

Vocabulary check

1. Money you receive if you lose your job and are out of work. *unemployment benefit*
2. A risk-taker in business is referred to as an *entrepreneur*.
3. The difference between a student loan and a *grant/scholarship* is that the former has to be repaid.
4. A student will try to *gain* work experience.
5. Students' dining facility at a college. *canteen, refectory*
6. Americans divide the academic year into two semesters, the British often have three *terms*.
7. A modern term for worker. *employee*
8. A student who gains a degree studying alone via media. *extramural student*, *correspondent student, long-distance learner*
9. Subjects a student is obliged to do are *compulsory*.
10. A syllabus can be part of a *curriculum*.
11. The results you need in order to enter a university in the U.K. *A Levels*

12. In order to get a degree after four/five years' study you need to write a *dissertation*.
13. The school leaving cert in America is the *High School Diploma*.
14. A written paper which a student has to do as part of a course. *assignment*
15. The long-term unemployed may receive *income support (BE), welfare (aid) (AE)*.
16. The head of the faculty. *dean*
17. The process of entering a university. *enrolment, matriculation*, etc.
18. Head of a college/university. *vice-chancellor, president*
    - ▶ Note: *The position of chancellor is normally an honorary position that entails no administration elements.*
19. Specially-built accommodation for students. *halls of residence, dormitory, student hostel*
20. A written work needed in order to get a doctorate. *doctoral thesis*

14 EXPRESSING TIME REFERENCES

▶ Note: The introductory rhyme uses the old English spelling *hath* of *have.*

Today is Thursday, 22 April

1. April 20 was *the day before yesterday*.
2. April 30 is *a week on Friday/tomorrow*.
3. An important exam for Lisa in December took place *five months ago*
4. Hazel had to go to the dentist on April 8, that was *two weeks/a fortnight ago*.
5. April last year was *last April*.
6. Next month is May. June is *the month after next*.
7. Next week, on Thursday, is *a week on Thursday*.
8. John Brennan attends many meetings. A staff meeting on April 18 took place *the other day/a few days ago/recently*.
9. A conference in February took place *a couple of/a few months ago*.
10. A discussion with trade union representatives in January was held *three months ago* while wage negotiations with employers in July will be held *in three months' time*.
11. Lisa's birthday will be on this exact date in May, i.e. *next month*.

SONG – FLIGHT OF EARLS

15

This song is included to give the book more of an Irish feeling. At the same time it is a useful gap-filling listening activity. *Flight of Earls* is a typical Irish folk song with lyrics focussing on social issues and was written at a time when unemployment in Ireland was very high. This situation has now reversed itself with Ireland's emergence as a centre for new technologies.

As a follow-up activity students should be asked to inform themselves and comment on the current situation regarding Ireland and compare this with their own country.

▶ Note: The signpost is written in Irish and English, illustrating the presence of both languages in everyday life. U2 is Ireland's biggest group. Bono is their lead singer. Guinness and whiskey are the national drinks of Ireland and major export earners.

Flight of Earls (Dublin City Ramblers)

I can hear the bells of Dublin in this lonely waiting room and the paper boys are singing in the rain, not too long before they take us to the airport and the noise, to get on board a *transatlantic* plane.

We've got nothing left to stay for, we have no more left to say, and there isn't any work for us to do. So farewell you boys and girls, another bloody Flight of Earls. Our best *asset* is our best export too.

It's not murder, fear or famine that makes us leave this time, we're not going to join McAlpines Fusilieres. We've got *brains* and we've got vision, we've got *education* too, but we just can't throw away these precious years.

So we walk the streets of London, and the streets of Baltimore and we meet at night in *several* Boston bars. We're the leaders of the future but we're far away from home, and we *dream* of you beneath the Irish stars.

As we look on Ellis Island and the Lady in the Bay, and Manhattan turns to face another Sunday. We just *wonder* what you're doing to bring us all back home as we look forward to another Monday. Because it's not the work that scares us, we don't mind an *honest* job, and we know things will get better once again.

So a thousand times adieu, we've got Bono and U2, all we're missing is the Guinness and the rain. So *switch off* your new computers because the writing is on the wall, we're leaving as our fathers did before. Take a look at Dublin Airport or the boat that leaves North Wall, there'll be no youth *unemployment* anymore.

Because we're over here in Queensland and in parts of New South Wales, we're on the *seas* and *airways* and the trains. But if we see better days, those big *airplanes* go both ways and we'll all be coming back to you again.

16 – 22 **Vocabulary**

▶ Note: You will come across the abbreviations *BE* and *AE* throughout the book. *BE* stands for *British English*, AE for *American English*.

Story Line

Hazel starts attending the Young Entrepreneurs' course which she finds very useful. In this unit she attends lectures on the internal organisation of a business as well as on types of business organisations. The information helps her to decide what type of business organisation would best suit her and how to structure her own firm.

Focus

- To enable students to follow a lecture and take appropriate notes
- To introduce students to different types of business organisations, company structures and departmental responsibilities

▶ Note: This is an important unit as it introduces basic business concepts which will be essential for the simulation in Unit 3 (Setting up a business) and the whole course. Make sure that students learn the vocabulary.

INTERNAL ORGANISATION *23 – 27*

Ask learners to open their books (p. 27) and to answer the comprehension questions while listening to the text. Play the cassette/CD twice and check answers. Alternatively, you can play the piece once, check comprehension and ask the students to read the text again at home and to complete/fill in the missing information, especially details regarding functions.

Comprehension *27*

A.

1. Prof. McMahon usually works in the Economics Faculty at Trinity College.
2. Prof. McMahon is giving her lecture instead of Phil Jennings whose lecture on Types of Business Organisations had to be postponed.
3. It is about the Internal Structure of Business.
4. It depends on the size and type of the firm.
5. The Board of Directors governs the company and decides on company policy, appoints the Managing Director/CEO.
6. The Chairperson or President.
7. His/Her job is to look after the day-to-day running of the business as well as to ensure that the policies decided by the board are carried out. The heads of department report to him/her.

8.

Manager	Dept./ Divn.	Functions
1st Chief Accountant	• Accounts Department	concerned with all payments, invoices wages, credit control, preparation of company accounts, drawing up budgets, forecasts, statistics
2nd Marketing Manager	• Market research	to find out the demand for a product and its chances on the market
	• Advertising	to inform about products, to persuade people to buy
	• Distribution and Sales	to ensure that customers get the product
3rd Company Secretary	• Administration Department	to co-ordinate activities and to provide services to other departments, e.g. data inputting, handling mail, secretarial and computing services, centralised filing
	• Legal Department	to ensure that company acts according to the law, deals with contracts, guarantees, insurance, compensation
4th Production Manager	• Production Department	to manufacture the products, to plan and organise production, quality control, to deal with complaints and faulty goods
5th Personnel Manager	• Personnel Department	to select and recruit and dismiss staff, to implement redundancy programs, to maintain personnel records, to provide references, to look after staff welfare, to organise training programs
6th Purchasing Manager	• Purchasing Department	to buy all raw materials, equipment and supplies, to deal with quotations, orders, deliveries, responsible for efficient stock-control system
	• Transport Department	to arrange delivery of goods
	• Research and Development	to develop new products and processes

28 **Exercises/Discussion**

1. Point out to students that *responsible to* and *for* are not the same, e.g. *I am a sales assistant, so I am responsible to the Sales Manager* (he's my boss) and *responsible for selling* (that's my task or job).

3. Possible answers:
   Chief Accountant: prompt payment of invoices by customers, to avoid bad debts;
   Personnel Manager: to employ most suitable staff;

Company Secretary: to ensure smooth running of the company, avoid court cases for the company;
Production Manager: to produce efficiently and without delays;
Purchasing Manager: to get the right goods at the right time at the right price.

TYPES OF BUSINESS ORGANISATIONS

28 – 31

Hazel's Notes

When working on the listening comprehension exercises students should be encouraged to use abbreviations and structure their notes appropriately. Hazel's notes serve as an example of how this could be done.

Ask the students to study Hazel's notes and do the presentation exercise, p. 29. Information about the structure of presentations as well as useful words and phrases can be found on pp. 282-84.

▶ Note: There are, of course, different regulations concerning business organisations in different countries – what is given here is only a brief overview.

Exercises

32

This exercise is quite demanding. Students may want to use their dictionaries, although the words needed to fill the gaps are all in the vocabulary list.

▶ Note: for one = on their part

1. headquarters – board of directors – commitment – balance sheet – CEO (because Martha Fowler works with the other departments) – implement – achieve – redundancies – to go public – debt – small-scale enterprise – takeover – bankruptcy – subordinates – shortage – approve – run.

2. A) Hazel has to *make* up her mind about the type of business organisation she wants.
   B) I've got so much work to *do* today.
   C) Always *do* the best you can.
   D) The Irish economy is *making* great progress at the moment.
   E) IBM is *doing* a lot of advertising at the moment.
   F) We can meet tomorrow. Let's *make* it for five.
   G) $400 is too low. I've got to *make* some profit on the deal!
   H) We *do* a lot of business in the Far East.

UNIT 3 THE BUSINESS PLAN

Story Line

Hazel was supposed to hand in the business plan to John Brennan in the Jobcentre. Her social life initially interfered with this but she finally got down to it. She also used the chance of getting some advice from Mr Wilkins, a bank manager and the father of her best friend Joan.

Focus

- To understand, formulate and present a business plan
- To introduce the simulation activity with the aim of consolidating vocabulary learned in the first three units
- To practise Social English in a relatively formal situation

40 BUSINESS PLAN GUIDELINES

For more detailed information on business plans please refer to the Internet links for this unit.

The guidelines represent the key points for a business plan as required by government and financial institutions in Ireland and the UK when applying for government support or credits. The ten points should be gone through very carefully by the students. Some of the points may be worth discussing in more detail, e.g. current market potential under Product/Service Description, the factors influencing the location for Physical Facilities (subsidies, infrastructure, skilled workforce) or what makes a good Management Team.

Marketing and advertising are covered in the following two units. At this stage the students should at least be made aware of the importance of focussing on a certain target group or groups for their goods/services and having good advertising ideas. The instructors may wish to read through Units 4 and 5 beforehand to help provide their learners with ideas.

For the section on Financial Projections it is standard for entrepreneurs to calculate over a twelve-month period on how much they would expect to receive from sales. Against that they have to calculate the cost of production, which includes materials, wages as well as rent, heating, electricity, telephoning, bank charges, etc.

HAZEL'S BUSINESS PLAN

41 – 42

Ask the students to take the paragraph headlines 1–10 of Business Plan Guidelines (p. 40) and insert them into Hazel's Business Plan (A–J) (pp. 41–42).

1. C	3. I	5. G	7. A	9. J
2. E	4. F	6. H	8. D	10. B

▶ Note: The IDA (Industrial Development Authority) is the Irish government agency responsible for furthering the development of industry. Its principal objective is to stimulate job creation by providing a range of financial and other services and incentives to support strategic growth in Irish companies and to attract international investment into Ireland. The USA is their main focus – Ireland with only 2% of the EU population accounts for over 35% of American investment in the EU.

MEETING MR WILKINS

43

Social English

Students often don't realise that they have problems using Social English appropriately in a relatively private situation. This is the focus of this exercise – role-plays follow on p. 44. Follow the instructions in the coursebook and play the cassette/CD. Afterwards, you may wish to compare the language style with the Jobcentre dialogue in Unit 1 (p. 11).

Mr W: How nice *to see you*, Hazel! Do come in.
H: Thank you. *Nice to see you* too, Mr Wilkins.
Mr W: Ahh ... come on now, Hazel, you can *call me* Michael. The bank is closed! Joan, darling, Hazel's here.
J: Hi Hazel.
H.: Hey Joan, how's life? Oh, by the way Mr Wilk ... I mean ... Michael, I've brought you a little *something*.
Mr W: Ahh ... a bottle of Bordeaux ... . You shouldn't have, but *thanks very much*.
H: That's OK.
Mr W: By the way, *how are* your parents?
H: *Fine*, thanks. They said to say hello. My Dad said that he'd give you a ring to organise a game of golf sometime.
Mr W: Great! I *look forward* to that. So, please, *have* a seat. Now, what *can I* get you ladies to drink before we have dinner? Hazel?

H: I'll have a whiskey and red, on the rocks.
J: And I'll _go for_ a dry martini.
Mr W: So Hazel, tell me, how is your business plan going so far?
H: It's going OK. I've got it here. I wonder if you could have a look at it for me before I hand it in, only if you have time.
Mr W: _Of course_.
H: There's one more thing. I have some questions concerning my financial requirements.
Mr W: No problem. I can arrange an _appointment_ at the bank. Let me see. When would be suitable for you? What about ...

44 1. A. Yes, it is./It sure is.
B. Not at all./Don't mention it./My pleasure.
C. Thank you./Glad you enjoyed it.
D. Nice to see you too.
E. Fine,/Very well, thanks. (**Not:** Thanks, very well.)/Not too bad./So-So./Could be worse./ Not too good, I'm afraid. And you?
F. Thank you, I'd love to./Thank you, that sounds very nice./I'm afraid I can't make it. Perhaps another time./I'd love to, but I've got another engagement.
G. How do you do? (I'm ...)
H. You're welcome./My pleasure.
I. No, not at all./Of course not./Go ahead./I'd rather you didn't.
J. Of course. Here you are.
K. You're welcome./My pleasure.
L. Never mind./It doesn't matter./Don't worry./Not to worry.
M. Yes. Here you are./I'm afraid I don't./Sorry, I don't smoke.

2. ▶ Note: *their* (in the task) is the neutral equivalent of *his/her*. Using only the *he* or *his* form is not seen as politically correct (PC).

Please make sure students cover the section dealing with Social English in the Reference Section (pp. 289–295). They should also discuss cultural differences such as the use of first names, bringing appropriate gifts or the acceptability of alcohol (see also Unit 11, pp. 199–202, 206–208).

45 4. Sample Solution
starting – entrepreneur – aware – service – gap – support – premises/property – employ – type – options – joint stock – person – solicitor (▶ Note: "lawyer" in AE) – clarify/consider – advice – financial records – require – accountant – setting – venture

Simulation 45

This page introduces the Simulation concept and outlines the simulation activities from Units 3–15. It is highly recommended to attempt at least this first simulation. The blank business plan form should be used by the students.

Tips for a successful simulation

The enterprise should be medium to large-sized so that each student is involved, i.e. responsible for one or more areas or departments in the organisation. Otherwise students should be allowed to be as creative as possible. Some students of ours came up with the idea of a funeral undertaker's, another group formed a company producing an expanding shoe. Other ideas were an IT magazine, a catering service, an ice-cream parlour chain, a mountain bike firm, a record company and a fashion accessory manufacturer.

This activity should be given enough time but setting a time limit is important.

Suggested approach:

1st session:

Approximately 45 minutes to get started, to discuss the business idea and responsibilities (i.e. who is the MD, who is responsible for which department(s), who would take care of which parts of the business plan). The students may also be asked to develop an organigram/company profile similar to the one on p. 25 of the Students' Book. Then group members work out their (individual) responsibilities in class or at home.

2nd session:

Approximately 45 minutes to work in groups discussing and fine-tuning material and preparing for group presentation. Please make sure that students refer to Presentations in the Reference Section (pp. 282–284). Afterwards group members present their project. All group members should be involved in the oral presentation. For example, the Managing Director might present the company profile on behalf of the whole group to the class while the department managers give a short presentation of their department(s) and responsibilities. If time is pressing each group member should only be allotted 2–3 minutes for presenting his/her part. In any event the business plan simulation should be completed by the end of the 3rd session.

The other students represent the audience and should be encouraged to ask questions afterwards. A government committee (perhaps consisting of one member of each group) could also be formed to decide which business idea merits government support.

▶ Note: If there is no time for the simulation in Unit 4, we suggest that students at least attempt the SWOT analysis part at this point in time. (See simulation notes in Unit 4 of this guide.)

If students have lots of time, they can set up their own home page for their business.

48 TWO POEMS FROM TWO STUDENTS

You may ask students to write their own poem as homework or as an end-of-class activity. It's a lot of fun and shows students are more creative than you might think!

Story Line

The opening song captures Hazel's thoughts of that summer – the sights, the smells, the sounds of Dublin. She is now in the middle of the course and dealing with the subject she knows least about – marketing. She's also got to devise a marketing plan for her own business.

Focus

- To develop reading skills
- To get a basic understanding of the tenets of marketing
- To enable students to describe trends and present graphs and figures

SONG: SUMMER IN DUBLIN 53

This song was chosen because it captures the essence of life in the centre of Dublin in the summer. It also serves as a counterbalance to a fairly intensive, theoretical self-study unit. When listening to the song students attempt the gap-filling exercise although they may find it difficult. They should be told beforehand that they are not expected to fill in all the gaps.

▶ Note: The photograph shows O'Connell Street Bridge, Dublin, on the River Liffey, Dublin's tidal river. Grafton Street is a pedestrian area and one of Dublin's most important shopping streets. 46A is a bus number operated by Dublin Bus. Dun Laoire is a major ferry port 11km from the centre of Dublin.

Summer in Dublin

Take me away from the city and leave me to where I can be *on my own*, I wanted to see you and now that I have I just want to be left alone. I'll always *remember* your kind words and I'll still remember your name but *I've* seen you changing and turning and I know that things just won't be the same.

Chorus: I remember that summer in Dublin and the Liffey as it stank like hell, and the young people walking on Grafton *Street* and everyone looking so well. I was singing a song I'd heard somewhere called 'Rock' n' Roll never forgets' when my humming was smothered by a *46A* and the scream of a *low-flying* jet. So I jumped on a bus to Dun Laoire stopping off to pick up my guitar and a drunk on the bus told me how to get rich. I was glad we weren't going too far.

So I'm leaving on Wednesday morning and trying to find a *place* where I can hear ... the wind and the birds and the sea on the rocks and where open roads always are near. And if sometime I tire of the *quiet* and I want to walk back up that *hill*, I'll just get on a road and I'll stick out my *thumb* because I know for sure that you'll be there still ...

Repeat Chorus

I remember that summer in Dublin ...

PRACTICAL MARKETING

This is an opportune time to introduce Reading Strategies (see Reference Section, p. 301) with the handbook format serving as a good introduction to reading Business Studies texts in English. Ask the students to read through the sections of the Practical Marketing material as a self-study exercise and then to answer the comprehension questions on p. 59.

59 Comprehension

1. Marketing is the process by which the demand for goods and services is anticipated (Market Research) and satisfied through the implementation of various marketing steps.
2. Marketing Mix stands for the four principal marketing variables (Product, Price, Promotion, Place). Product Mix is the range of products offered by a company.
3. Branding means applying the company's 'signature' to its products by using special names, symbols or signs.
4. Packaging does not only protect the product but has also the function of attracting the customer and reinforcing the brand image. This is of particular importance in today's competitive world. For environmentally conscious people excessive packaging may have a negative impact on their willingness to buy.
5. The product life cycle starts off with the introductory phase (product is launched), followed by the growth phase. In the maturity phase sales are stabilising and competitive products enter the market with the effect that marketing efforts have to be increased. Then there is the saturation phase, i.e. the target customers have bought the product, which is followed by the decline – sales are falling. Product harvesting can start, i.e. the product is sold without any further advertising or marketing expenditures.
6. Price plateau is the price level that is expected by customers, penetration pricing involves charging a low price when a new product/service is launched in order to gain market share, creaming means setting a higher price which is accepted because the product is new.

7. These are advertising, personal selling, sales promotion and publicity.
8. Advertising is the promotion of goods and services through various media forms using the spoken and printed word as well as visual means. Sales promotion (indirect advertising) tries to stimulate sales by the use of incentives such as trading stamps, free samples and competitions.
9. It is the shortest and therefore the cheapest way.
10. You can sell a product in certain shops at a higher price, e.g. because there is a high demand for this particular product, e.g. hot beverages in a skiing area or clothes from an exclusive boutique.
11. Because one can adapt a marketing strategy/marketing mix to the requirements of this particular group of people who have a common need or desire for a certain product.
12. These are geographical, demographic and buyer behaviour.
13. As marketing and advertising is done by all companies, customers are in a position to inform themselves and choose the products they like best. On the other hand, the competition between firms has a positive impact on the quality of goods.
    Good market research reduces the risk of offering a product that does not sell well.
14. The four keys state that you should specialise in a certain product or a limited number of products which should be different from those of your competitors. You have to find your market segment where you can become the market leader if you concentrate your resources and work hard enough.

THE MARKETING PLAN *60*

The text can be used as an extra reading practice or as a preparation for the following simulation activity.

Inform students that corporate objectives can refer to the type of products or services the organisation plans to offer, the raising of efficiency levels, social responsibility, profit maximisation, number of staff needed, etc, while marketing objectives can refer more specifically to market share, product quality etc.

For more detailed information on marketing please refer to the Internet links provided for this unit.

61 **Simulation**

The students may find this simulation more challenging than the business plan. A blank marketing plan form is provided on p. 62.

As a preparation the students could be encouraged to imagine what the typical marketing plan of a multinational company such as Coca-Cola or a small neighbourhood firm is like. Alternatively students can use the home page links or surf the Internet. If there is no time for a full simulation, we suggest that students at least attempt the SWOT analysis part for their business (if this has not already been done as part of the business plan project in Unit 3).

You may wish to help your students out with the points below but the participants should first try to discuss them among themselves.

Sample answers for SWOT section of the marketing plan (p. 61):

Strengths of a business:
High-quality products
Experienced management
Efficient distribution system
State of the art technology

Weaknesses:
Average age of management
High labour costs
Inability to raise finance
High research and development costs if some products are in decline phase

Opportunities:
New markets opening up
Little or no competition
Government support
Cheaper raw materials

Threats:
New competitors entering market
Higher fuel and energy prices
General recession
Excessive wage demands
Restrictive government legislation

Alternatively ask your students to prepare a SWOT analysis on their home town, the objective being to making it a destination of choice for living, education, business or tourism.

Exercises/Discussion 63

1. It is helpful to put the spidergram on the board and get the students to give answers. These could include:

   price
   quality
   reliability
   guarantees
   image of the company
   promotion of the product
   brand image
   fashionability
   up-to-dateness
   appearance
   loyalty, etc.

2. No. Refer to the section on price (p. 56).

3. Some arguments could be that the customers are influenced by the brand image (e.g. young, bold, exclusive), or are convinced of the superior quality of the branded product.

4. It is commonly believed that every *firm* should have a marketing *plan*, otherwise it will not achieve its marketing *objectives*. In today's world effective market *research* is a necessary precondition. Some marketing *specialists* see direct marketing as the ultimate solution as it *enables* the seller to identify *consumer* needs.

   Think of the *junk mail* from companies filling your letterbox, much of it offering free offers or special prizes when all that they want is to gather as much *data* on you as possible. Or think of those *cold calls* in the evenings, and direct marketing seems a nightmare. But this is definitely a move away from *mass* marketing towards a more information-led, one-to-one marketing *approach*.

   The low costs of direct marketing have created a huge and fast-growing *industry* which is made up of direct mail, *telemarketing*, database marketing, the Internet, freephone numbers and print advertisements.

▶ Note: Direct marketing is the use of direct communications such as mail, catalogues, telemarketing, etc at carefully targeted consumers in order to obtain an immediate response.

64 5. 1 – d (market research); 2 – i (life cycle); 3 – k (pie chart); 4 – f (brand loyalty); 5 – c, n (product mix, name); 6 – e (distribution channel); 7 – l (purchasing power); 8 – m, n (trade fair, name); 9 – j (advertising budget); 10 – b (mass market); 11 – c, j (marketing mix, budget); 12 – b (target market); 13 – a (sales promotion); 14 – h (competitive advantage)

65 PRESENTING GRAPHS AND FIGURES

It's imperative that students are given time to go through Describing Trends in the Reference Section (pp. 304–305). This is an important aspect of business especially when giving presentations of sales figures, reports, etc.

1.

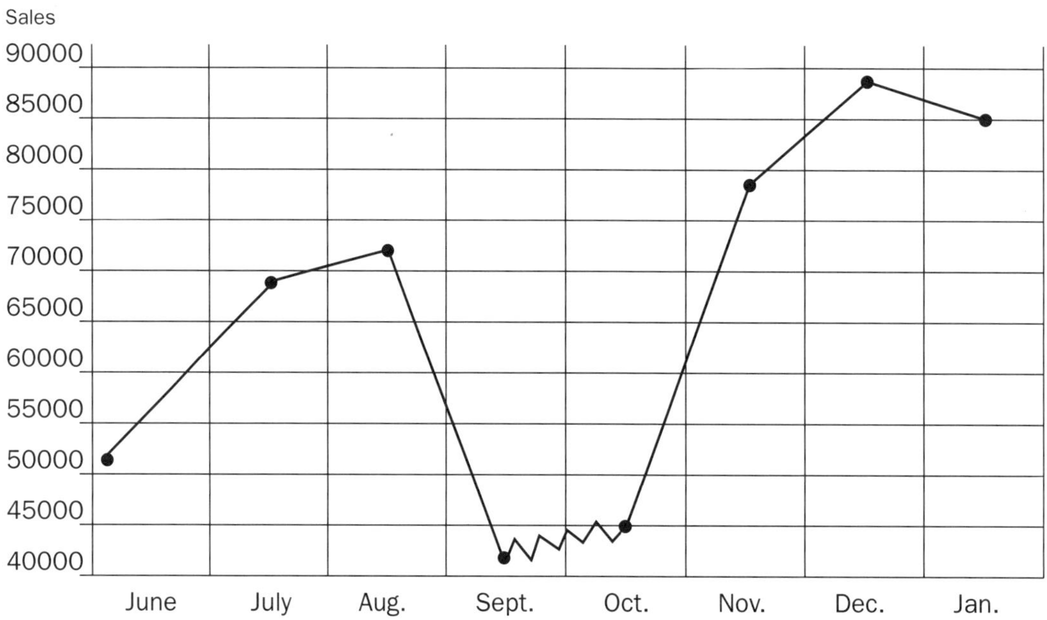

2.

Month	Reason
June	Ad campaign
July	Increased summer demand
August	New contract with IDO
September	Strong British pound
October	Increasing demand NZ & Australia
November	New product range launched

4. Students are expected to discuss which answers are appropriate. All are applicable except e). 66

5. See Reference Section, p. 305. It is a useful exercise to get students to write a description of the graph. In addition ask them to bring in a graph sample from the newspapers and describe it in detail so that the others can draw it on a sheet of paper or on the board. This is also possible as pair work. 67

UNIT 5 ADVERTISING

Story Line

Hazel is attending a presentation on advertising given by a Dr Robertson and later designs an ad for her new company Celtic Design Jewellery Ltd for a trade journal. Her company is almost ready to start trading.

Focus

- To introduce and practise the language of presentations
- To develop listening for specific information and gist by following a presentation on advertising
- To discuss the world of advertising including an advertisement workshop activity

73 A PRESENTATION ON ADVERTISING

Presentations remain one of the most common and challenging aspects of business activities particularly for newcomers. Dr Robertson's presentation represents an everyday standard.

Take your learners through the part on Presentations in the Reference Section, pp. 282–284. Students open books and read introduction to the unit. Leave books open for the following listening comprehension tasks (A and B).

Dr. Robertson's Presentation

A. INTRODUCTION

'So *good morning, everybody*, I'm Dr Robertson and I am currently the managing director of Peters and Dunne, the well-known Anglo-Irish advertising agency. I'd like *to thank you all* for being here.

My purpose today is to talk to you about advertising. As you know, advertising is a vital part of marketing, and we come into contact with advertising almost every day of our lives. *I intend to divide* my talk into four main parts. First of all I will tell you about the different types of advertising, and *afterwards* have a brief look at the work of the advertising agencies. Then I would like *to move on* to discuss advertising media and promotion activities and finally *finish up* on the recent trend towards 'yobbish' advertising. At the very end I would briefly like to go over the advantages for entrepreneurs and the general public. *If you have any questions*, I'll be happy to try and answer them at the end of my talk. OK, *let me explain* what advertising is.

It can be defined as the promotion of goods and services through various media forms. The primary objective of advertising is, of course, to increase sales and profits.

Now, _as you can see_ from my first transparency, there are six main types of advertising. By the way, there's no need to take them down as they are all in the _handouts_ on your desks'.

2. Greeting, introducing oneself, introducing the topic, giving a short outline of the talk, stating when questions are welcome, referring to visual aids.

See also Reference Section on Presentations, pp. 282-84, for more detailed information.

B. TYPES OF ADVERTISING

74

'The first type listed is *informative advertising* which informs people about the _availability_ of a product or service, its _features_ and its _price_. On another level, the government uses informative advertising in order to educate and to advise people, as you may have noticed from the recent Aids Awareness campaign.

The second one is *persuasive advertising* which not only informs people about products or services but also tries to _persuade_ people to buy, through the use of special techniques, especially _psychological_ ones. It tends to focus on the _image_ created rather than on the actual product. This type of advertising is the most _dominant_ today and is widely used in the sales of cosmetics, narcotics, alcohol and of almost any other product. A famous example is the Marlboro Man campaign. By the way, the original Marlboro Man died of lung cancer!

The next type is *generic advertising*. It is often employed by an industry or trade association with the objective of promoting the products of that _particular industry_ . An example is the National Dairy Council with their 'Drink more milk' media campaign. It should be clearly understood that they are promoting milk in _general_ on behalf of all the dairy companies and not an individual brand.

Reminder advertising has the object of informing the public that the product or service is *still available*. In other words, it helps keep it in their *minds*. It's sometimes referred to as 'tickle advertising'.

The fifth one, *reinforcement advertising*, is used by firms that are facing new competition. They seek to *assure* their existing customers that they have made the *correct decision* by choosing their products and that there is no need to try or switch to the newly launched product. Alternatively, they may highlight the risk of changing to another brand.

Finally, we come to *comparative advertising* or *competitive advertising* as it is often known. This form is widespread in the United States and tries to *convince* the public that one company's product is better than its competitors by *comparing* price, features, etc. It was forbidden, until recently, in most other countries including all the countries in the European Union.'

74 2. Good examples of comparative or competitive advertising are Pepsi and Coca Cola or McDonalds and Burger King. Students should be able to find examples for other types of advertising.

Another form of advertising is referred to as contact advertising. Here, two different products from the same organisation are promoted. A good example is Diageo PLC with its TV commercial promoting both Foster's (beer) and Häagen-Dazs (ice-cream) together.

76 **C. ADVERTISING AGENCIES**

For this listening activity make sure that the students close their books and take notes.

1. Functions of Advertising agencies: Market Research, Media Planning, Advertising Planning, Production of Advertisements, Advertising Consultancy.

D. ADVERTISING MEDIA AND SALES PROMOTION ACTIVITIES

First of all make sure that students know the difference between Advertising Media (TV, newspapers, etc) and Sales Promotion activities (special offers, free gifts, etc). They have already covered the difference between the two in Unit 4, p. 57.

1. In this part of his presentation Dr Robertson refers to two diagrams which the students see as empty boxes. Before listening, students should be asked to fill the diagrams listing: *76*

* all advertising media – (Diagram 1): radio and TV, newspapers and magazines, cinema, trade fairs and exhibitions, neon signs, posters, internet, product endorsement, balloons, product placement, window displays, product wrapping, trade journals.

* all sales promotion activities – (Diagram 2): special offers, trading stamps and coupons, sponsorship, direct mailing, personality promotion, loss leaders, samples, free gifts, free draws, competitions.

Alternatively this exercise can be done on the board involving the whole class. Then listen and complete the missing information. Finally check their answers in the text, pp. 78–79.

E. TRENDS AND BENEFITS *79*

If this is to be done as a listening exercise ask your learners to keep their books closed. The five questions in Exercise 1 should be put on the board, an overhead transparency or dictated before commencing the exercise. You may, however, want your students to read the last section if you find the listening exercise too long.

1.

a. Ambition, success, romance, hero worship, desire for an easier life.
b. The consumer knows exactly how advertising works.
c. These are the trends towards more violence, crude images, bad language, yobbish advertising, but also more creativity.
d. The examples mentioned are the Great Frog Jewellery commercial where a girl gives the ‘finger’ and vulgar language is used, the advertising campaign from McVities with the slogan “Kill all Barbie Dolls”, and the Dudley Moore movie where inmates of a mental institution are hired to create crazy ads, which turns out to be a great success.

e. Advertising informs consumers about products, it's an industry that provides jobs, keeps prices of certain articles like newspapers down, promotes healthy competition and makes the world more colourful.

81 **Discussion**

Here students have the opportunity to discuss different aspects of advertising.

2. Negative aspects of advertising are, for example, that it makes people greedy, it is a waste of resources, creates unreal needs, may have a negative impact on children, encourages crime among poorer sections of the community in order to pay for products/ services advertised, advertising expenditures increase the price of a product, source of irritation, etc.

Workshop Activity

The instructor should bring along some sample advertisements from newspapers, magazines, posters and other print media in order to introduce and discuss the advertisement assessment criteria (p. 81).

▶ Note: *Methods/techniques used* refers to psychological techniques, use of colour, women, people, pets, etc. *Information/product benefits emphasised* refers to price, place, qualities, ingredients, performance, etc.

Optional Video Activity:

The advertisement assessment criteria can also be used to assess pre-recorded TV commercials.

82 A. This exercise provides an opportunity to practise the language of advertising and can be done either in writing or as pair work activity.

Exercises B and C are ideal homework activities, the presentation of which can be done after The Language of Presentations (pp. 83-85) for practice and consolidation purposes.

83 **Vocabulary check**

1. A short word for advertisement. *ad/vert*
2. This unit deals with the study of *advertising* not advertisement.
3. A short advertisement text line. *caption/slogan*
4. Type of advertising that uses psychological techniques. *persuasive*
5. An ad on TV. *commercial*
6. A hoarding is referred to as a *billboard* in the USA.

7. Advertising material that's more detailed than a leaflet. *brochure*
8. Firms which specialise in planning advertising campaigns for firms. *advertising agencies*
9. PR stands for *Public Relations*.
10. The act where a household name, i.e. a well-known person, approves a product or service. *endorsement*
11. Another term for direct mail. *junk mail*
12. Advertising done by an industry or trade association. *generic*
13. Leipzig and Hanover are famous for this type of event. *trade fair*
14. To interest or be attractive to. *appeal*
15. A synonym for starting an advertising campaign. *launching*

83 THE LANGUAGE OF PRESENTATIONS

The following exercises focus on important aspects of presentations.

A. INTRODUCING A PRESENTATION

4. What I'd like to talk about today is ...
7. The aim of this presentation is ...
14. Today, I'm going to talk about ...

B. SEQUENCING

12. Secondly ...

C. REFERRING TO TEXT/VISUALS

8. As you can see from this graph ...
9. Now, let's look at the transparency ...
11. This pie chart shows ...
13. To illustrate this point I'd like you to look at this graph ...
16. A good example of this is shown in your handouts ...

D. CHANGING TOPIC

2. The next ...
3. Let me turn now to ...
5. Right, I've told you about all the ...
15. Let's move on to part ...

E. CONCLUDING

1. Let me remind you finally of the main points I covered.
5. Right, I've told you about all the ...
6. So, to conclude let me ...
10. In conclusion, we can say ...

b) Students should be made aware that intensifiers are necessary to emphasise important pieces of information. The answers should be read aloud in order to stress the intensifiers. 85

Sample Key (Variations are possible in the answers.)

1. really
2. extremely
3. really/just
4. strongly
5. so
6. far too
7. quite
8. just/only
9. certainly

Simulation

In this simulation students are afforded the opportunity of developing and presenting an advertising strategy for their business and/or design an ad. If the original business project cannot be continued (because old groups no longer exist or have altered membership), the new groups will have to agree on a product and type of enterprise first.

This simulation can be done either in class as a group project (in a 90-minute period) or as a more extensive activity where each group member develops a strategy and/or designs an ad at home, then presents it to his/her group. The best strategy/ad is then selected and refined for a presentation to the whole class.

Story Line

Hazel has an appointment with Mr Wilkins at Standard Irish Bank to discuss the financial requirements for her new business. Unfortunately he's busy so she talks to John Elliott who seems to take a fancy to her and grants her the necessary finance.

Her next appointment is with Bernard O'Regan at the Industrial Development Authority (government agency for promoting and assisting entrepreneurs). Hazel has already received government grants via the Jobcentre and is hoping to get a subsidised premises from the IDA. She is late and has to ring up a clearly annoyed Mr O'Regan who cancels the meeting but informs her that she meets the required conditions and will receive the keys of the premises at Summerhill Industrial Park very soon.

▶ Note: *Premises* can be used in singular or plural.

FOCUS

- To introduce students to the key aspects of banking
- To communicate effectively in standard banking situations such as opening a bank account and discussing a loan
- To develop students' telephoning skills

89 – 91 **AT THE BANK**

A. BANK PRODUCTS

This is a reading exercise where students are then expected to fill in a table (p. 92).

92 **Exercises/Discussion**

1. ▶ Note: A *credit card* is issued by a specialist finance company such as Visa or Mastercard while the *bank card* is issued by a commercial bank or a similar financial institution.

The bank card has the following functions:

- to withdraw money from an ATM (Automated Teller Machine, i.e. cash machine)
- to guarantee cheques
- to pay in stores, etc – the amount being debited immediately from the holder's current account – the debit card function
- a so-called 'smart' card facility where the holder can load up units of money on his/her bank card and pay in stores (similar to using a telephone card)

For *telephone banking* you need a telephone and a special identification code. 92
Instructions concerning transfers and payments are possible by phone. Cash withdrawals and lodgements (= payments in) are not possible. No computer equipment is necessary.

Advantages	Disadvantages
SAVINGS ACCOUNT	
easy to withdraw, low risk	*low interest rates*
DEPOSIT ACCOUNT	
higher interest rates	*capital must be left for fixed period*
CURRENT ACCOUNT	
instant withdrawals, cheque book (importance steadily decreasing), overdraft facility	*low or no interest* *bank charges*
BANK CARD	
cash from ATM, print statements, checks balances, wide acceptability	*easy to overspend*
TELEPHONE BANKING	
convenient, 24-hour-service	*security risk, restricted in scope, no face-to-face contact*
CREDIT CARD	
sometimes no annual fee, interest free short-term credit, necessary for e-commerce payments, sign of credibility	*easy to overspend, security risk (for payments via Internet), high interest rate*

2. Formerly known as home banking, internet/electronic (or online) banking requires access to the Internet and computer facilities. With Internet banking you have direct access to your account through various identification codes. Transfer and payment instructions can be given. Advantages are the same as in telephone banking. In addition to that, you can also see all your account details on screen. Disadvantages are similar to telephone banking as stated above.

3. Other services offered by banks include
   - Insurance
   - Securities trading
   - Safe deposit box facility
   - Financial advice including tax consultancy, investment and general financial information
   - Trustee services; the bank manages money or property for a person or persons, e.g. minors
   - Executorship services, which involves dealing with wills and settling people's affairs when they die
   - Foreign currency
   - International payment transfers

93 4.

1 – F	3 – B	5 – E	7 – A
2 – D	4 – C	6 – H	8 – G

94 5. ▶ Note: Although its use is declining due to electronic payments, the cheque is still fairly common in English-speaking countries.

Students tend to confuse the fact that this is a company cheque book and not a personal cheque book – Kathleen Burke is an employee with signing authority. The no. of this cheque is 001390.

a. 25 May 20..
b. Kathleen Burke
c. Martin Bolton
d. Comerfreight plc
e. Comerfreight plc
f. The Standard Irish Bank branch at 27 College Green, Dublin 2
g. Kathleen Burke made it out in favour of Martin Bolton.

h. Martin Bolton 94
i. 20-15-01 in the top right hand corner is the bank code
j. a/c = account (This is a standard question unconnected with the cheque.)

6. ▶ Note: The term *checking a/c* is American English for the British English *current a/c*.

This is a jumbled exercise with some solutions given. When arranged in the right order this dialogue can be used as the basis for an open role-play.

1. Hi, can I help you?
2. Yes, I'd like to open a checking account.
3. Are you a student?
4. No, I'm not. I'm a computer programmer at Dell Computers.
5. OK, here's an application form. Please fill it in.
6. Thanks.
7. Will you also be requiring our ConnectPlus? That's a combined cash, debit and cheque card.
8. Yes. It could come in useful. How long will I have to wait for it?
9. The card will take about eight working days to order. You'll receive your P.I.N. code in the mail.
10. (Later) Here's the completed form.
11. OK. Thanks. Can you please show proof of identity and proof of your current permanent address?
12. Sure, here's my driving license and my latest household electric bill.
    ▶ Note: A household bill is accepted as proof of current permanent address in English-speaking countries. Ireland, the UK and the USA have no ID cards and the passports do not contain citizens' addresses.
13. Fine. That's great. By the way, if you have any questions about our other products, don't hesitate to call Tom Barry, our customer services officer.
14. OK. Thanks for the tip.
15. Have a nice day.
16. You too.

95 – 96 B. AT RECEPTION

Social English

L: Excuse me, Ms Browne. I'm afraid Mr Wilkins is still with a customer. He told me through the intercom that it may take another 15 minutes or so before he'll be through. *Do you mind waiting* ?

H: No, of course not.

L: Can I offer you some tea or coffee?

H: *No, thanks* .

(Twenty minutes later)

Mr W: Hazel, terribly sorry about this but there's a bit of a problem. I don't want to keep you waiting any longer, so I've arranged that Mr Elliott, one of our business loan officers, will speak to you or, if you like, *we could make a new appointment* ?

H: No, Mr Wilkins, Mr Elliott is fine.

Mr W: Linda, can you ask John to come to the counter?

L: Of course. (*Picks up the phone, dials John*) Hi, Linda here at reception. The manager would like to see you at the counter straight away. (*Turns to Mr Wilkins.*) *He's on his way* , Manager.

Mr W: Fine. Thanks ... Ah ... John ... there you are. I'd like you to meet Ms Browne.

JE: *How do you do*, Ms Browne.

H: *How do you do*, Mr Elliott.

Mr W: Ms Browne is starting up her own business and has certain financial requirements. *I'd like you to take care of her.* I was going to do it myself but I've been held up. Maguire from Cashel Developments is in with me at the moment. Anyhow, Hazel, if you have any questions, give me a call at home tonight. Again, apologies for this.

H: *It's really all right*, Mr Wilkins. Thanks a lot.

Mr W: OK then. Here's the file, John. The application forms are in there. Everything's approved. Just take her through the details.

JE: *Come this way, please.* My office is right through here.

98 C. DISCUSSING A LOAN

For most learners, this is a challenging listening comprehension exercise. Students should go through the comprehension questions (p. 98) prior to commencing the listening activity. Make sure that students don't read the transcript.

Comprehension 98

1. Working Capital is needed to keep the business running, to buy raw materials, pay wages, etc, whereas development capital is needed when setting up a business, e.g. to buy the premises and equipment.
2. A loan of € 90,000 and an overdraft facility of € 10,000.
3. She also gets a grant from the government.
4. It is valued at € 156,000 and serves as security for the loan.
5. The sum includes the principal plus interest and charges.
6. Set-up charges are levied for arranging the loan, administration charges for managing the loan for its duration.
7. It protects her against default, i.e. if she is unable to repay the loan as in the case of illness or death.
8. The payments can be rescheduled.
9. The rate of interest is influenced by the type of borrower, the type of business and the risk involved, the security provided and the period of the loan.
10. There is a always the risk that a business can go bankrupt resulting in bad debts.
11. Hazel is visiting the Industrial Development Authority which promotes industrial development by assisting home-based firms and by trying to attract foreign companies.

D. A LETTER FROM A BANK 99

The first task for the students is to read the letter and identify the problems which Ally (short for Alistair) McCoist faces. Ally has overdrawn his bank account but has not paid in anything since the overdraft limit was agreed. A letter from the bank regarding this problem has also been ignored by Ally. His overdraft limit has now been withdrawn and further steps will be undertaken by the bank if he does not contact them straightaway.

▶ Note: *APR* stands for *Annual Percentage Rate* (of charge) and represents the true cost of borrowing, i.e. interest plus administration costs. *Formal Demand* is a request for immediate and full repayment of the outstanding amount owed by the debtor.

Role-play

Students should be creative in explaining the reasons behind Ally's failure to repay the overdraft. This exercise can be done either as phone call or a face-to-face conversation. Students should therefore refer to Telephoning (pp. 287–288) and/or Looking at Options/ Proposals (p. 299) and Bargaining/Making Compromises (p. 300) in the Reference Section.

100 E. DESCRIBING TRENDS – LINKING DEVICES

Students choose the appropriate answer from the three possibilities given on each line in the box.

1. in order
2. Although
3. despite
4. but
5. still
6. Nevertheless
7. Moreover
8. and
9. While
10. In general
11. especially
12. Personally

F. TELEPHONING THE IDA

1. With books closed students note down the documents that have to be sent in by Hazel plus the appointment details.
   The bank's loan approval and a copy of the loan agreement have to be sent in.
   The appointment is at Hazel's new premises in Summerhill Industrial Park on Thursday 15, at 3pm where the keys will be handed over.

2. The aim of this exercise is to give students the chance to familiarise themselves with standard telephoning phrases. Please make sure they refer to both When You Make A Call (Hazel's part) and When You Receive A Call (Part for Receptionist and B. O' Regan) in the Reference Section (pp. 285–288) for this exercise.

R: Good afternoon, IDA, Reception, Christina Scully speaking – can I help you/ *What can I do for you*?
H: Yes, I'd like to speak to/*Can I speak to* Bernard O'Regan in the Small Business and Services Division.
R: Who may I say is calling/*Who's speaking please*?
H: Hazel Browne.
R: I'm afraid Mr O'Regan's line is engaged at the moment/*on a call*.
H: I understand/*I see*.

R: Would you like to hold/*Would you like to wait*? 101

H: Yeah ... OK.

(Three minutes later.)

R: OK, Ms Browne, putting you through/*transferring you through now*.

H: Thanks.

O'Regan: O'Regan speaking.

H: Hi, this is/*my name is* Hazel Browne. I'm ringing to let you know that/*I'm phoning because* I'm going to be late for our appointment. I'm really sorry. It's the traffic, you see ...

O'Regan: Ms Browne, it's almost four o'clock on a Friday afternoon. I don't plan to be in the office much longer.

H: Oh, I'm really sorry. Maybe we should make a new appointment.

O'Regan: Hmm ... To tell you the truth I'm really busy these days. Let me find your file to see what the story is. One moment please./*Could you hold on a moment please*?

H: No problem. *OK/Fine*.

O'Regan: Ahh ... here we go. Right then. Everything seems to be more or less OK. We've examined your proposal and your business plan. What I'm waiting for now is a copy of the bank's loan approval and a copy of the loan agreement.

H: OK. That'll be on the way soon.

O'Regan: Right. I don't think there'll be any need to come to my office but we'll need to arrange an appointment at your new premises in Summerhill Industrial Park to hand over the keys. When would suit you?

H: The best time for me is on a Thursday or Friday afternoon.

O'Regan: Fine, let's make it a Thursday afternoon at 3pm then. Not next Thursday, as I'll be away at a conference. The following Thursday ... that's the fifteenth. And try and be on time. Buy a watch, if you don't have one already. Anyhow, have a nice weekend.

H: OK. The same to you. And thanks again for your help/*Thank you very much for everything.*

O'Regan: You're welcome/*Not at all*, etc. Bye now/*Bye for now*/*See you soon.*

H: Bye.

102 3. Telephoning role-plays

Before attempting this exercise ask students to study both the introductory page to Telephoning and Numbers (pp. 303– 304) in the Reference Section. This is important as they will be asked to read out addresses, spell names and give telephone and fax numbers.

105 **Vocabulary check**

1. American term for current account. *checking a/c*
2. To take or *withdraw* money from an account.
3. What you earn on a savings a/c. *interest*
4. To lodge cash and cheques on an a/c. *pay in*
5. To withdraw more money than you have on your a/c. *overdraw*
6. American English synonym for security. *collateral*
7. To move money from one a/c to another. *transfer*
8. To send money by post to someone in payment for goods. *remit*
9. Person or organisation that owes a financial obligation. *debtor*
10. A printed record of transactions on a bank account. *statement*

Simulation

In this simulation it may be difficult to involve all the students. Those students who are not involved should comment on the authenticity of the simulation and the appropriateness of language use, errors, etc.

As an option more group members may be involved and asked to contact different banks with the aim of getting the best deal.

Story Line

Hazel has finally got the company started. Manufacturing has started, and she is really stressed. Despite this she's off to a wedding in Belgium. Gareth, an old friend of hers, is getting married. He lives in Brussels and works as an assistant for a British Labour Party MEP (Member of the European Parliament). So hiring the white-collar staff will have to wait. John Elliott, the bank loan officer, and her have had a short fling which she really doesn't want – another reason for a break.

Gareth is there to meet Hazel at Brussels Airport. They drop in at his office as he has some things to do. While he's sorting himself out she reads up on the EU and takes part in an argument between Gareth and Norman, his English colleague. Afterwards Gareth and Hazel explore Brussels and end up in an Irish pub before they go to a party organised by two Spanish girls.

Focus

- To extensively practise the language of business trips from booking a ticket to socialising
- To get an insight into and discuss the European Union

OFF TO BRUSSELS 111

The first exercise focuses on listening for numbers, figures and times.

A. RESERVING AND PAYING FOR THE PLANE TICKET

TA: So, if you stay over the *eighth*, that's the *Thursday* night – it will be a lot cheaper.

H: That's possible.

TA: OK then. Flying out on the 5th at *11.25* in the morning. Flight *LH 1258* ... eh ... I mean *1285*. Arriving in London at *12.10*.

H : OK, and then I change for Terminal 1, flight LH *4370* on to Brussels.

TA: Yes ... You'll be there at *15.40* local time. And returning on the 11th from Brussels via Manchester. Flight *744*. Now the price. That'll be *€ 283* plus *€ 19* tax. How would you like to pay?

H: I'll pay with my Visa card. The number is 4917 8720 6489 *0054*. It's really amazing, isn't it? A return is almost the same price as the *€ 217* single fare. Crazy.

TA: Yes, but remember that these *dates* and times are fixed. You cannot change them later as you're taking advantage of the lowest fares on offer.

H: OK. That's clear.

TA: I'll issue the tickets in the next *three* days.
H: Great. As long as I have them by the *twelfth*. I can have them collected. What are your opening times?
TA: Our business hours are Monday to Saturday *10.30* to *7pm* and Sundays from *12* to *2*.

105 **B. CHECKING IN**

This is a guided role-play where students get the chance to practise buying a ticket.

112 **Social English**

Students can check a variety of answers under Social English in the Reference Section.

Question/Comment	Response
Hi Gareth, how are you?	*Fine, and you?*
Congratulations on getting married!	*Thank you!*
Nice to see you again.	*Nice to see you too.*
It's been a long time!	*It sure has.*
Have you been to Brussels before, Hazel?	*Yes, I have./No, I haven't. It's my first time.*
And how was the weather in Dublin?	*Great./Very sunny/hot/good/cloudy/rainy/cold, etc.*
Hazel, thanks for the bottle of whiskey.	*You're welcome./Don't mention it.*
How are we going to get to the hotel?	*I've got my car with me./By taxi, bus, etc.*

AT THE EU HEADQUARTERS

The EU is constantly in a state of flux. This represents a good opportunity for students to supplement the material in this unit by checking out the latest developments in the media.

A. BACKGROUND

This is a reading exercise focusing on vocabulary. Another option is to ask your students to give a short oral summary of the text.

comprises = consists of
pooled = put together
common = collective
secure = dependable
implementing = enforcing
pursued = followed
effect = force
extra = additional
adopted = chosen
introduced = launched
settling = paying
perform = function
independent = self-governing

B. EURO HISTORY

116

Students listen to the text and fill in the information asked for. Afterwards check their answers with the transcript on the following page. Please ask students to cover p. 117 with a sheet of paper.

EURO HISTORY

1962 *European Commission proposed a single currency.*

1989 *Members agreed a three-stage timetable to establish a common currency.*

1992 *The Maastricht Treaty was signed.*

1993 *Introduction of a common and free market.*

1994 *Foundation of the European Monetary Institute. (Beginning of stage two.)*

1995 *Name for the new currency was agreed. (Mr Waigel's idea.)*

1996 *First banknotes were displayed.*

1997 *The coins were displayed. Legal guidelines for the employment of the new currency were passed.*

1998 *Eleven member countries reached the economic criteria for participation. European Central Bank started its work. (Stage three.)*

1999 *Introduction of the euro but national currencies still in use.*

2002 *Euro notes and coins replace national currencies.*

Criteria for participation: *Stable prices and exchange rates, fixed interest rates, the annual budget deficit should not exceed 3% of GDP or total national debt should not exceed 60% of GDP.*

Advantages: *Elimination of currency fluctuations and the multitude of currencies, enormous savings on banking transaction costs, euro can become a serious rival to the US dollar, consumers can compare prices, competition may bring prices down.*

118 **C. DISCUSSING THE EU**

Ask students to close their books for this listening exercise. They should then note down the speakers' pros or cons.

Pros:
- bigger market of over 320 million people
- less dependent on one country for trade
- poorer regions receive support
- wider range of consumer goods on offer
- equal rights for workers in EU
- studying abroad is much easier
- degrees are increasingly internationally recognised
- EU advice and support may help firms

Cons:
- a lot of people are against the EU
- trade links with other countries may be lost
- wealthier nations are net contributors to EU
- money is wasted, high membership costs
- EU is very bureaucratic, some regulations are ridiculous
- EU may become more powerful than national governments
- more and stiffer competition, bad especially for small businesses as euro favours big business

119 **Discussion/Vocabulary**

As an option 1 and 2 can be organised along the lines of a meeting (see pp. 296–298).

1. A further development of the last exercise where students focus on the pros and cons of EU membership for their particular country.

2. This may produce some heated arguments – appropriate language should be used – see phrases from the Language of Meetings (pp. 297–298).

3.

Country	Nationality	Person	Language(s)	Capital
Austria	Austrian	Austrian	German	Vienna
Belgium	Belgian	Belgian	Flemish/Dutch/ French	Brussels
Denmark	Danish	Dane	Danish	Copenhagen
Finland	Finnish	Finn	Finnish	Helsinki
France	French	Frenchman/ -woman	French	Paris
Germany	German	German	German	Berlin
Greece	Greek	Greek	Greek	Athens
Ireland	Irish	Irishman/ -woman	English/Irish Gaelic	Dublin
Italy	Italian	Italian	Italian	Rome

Country	Nationality	Person	Language(s)	Capital
Luxembourg	Luxembourg	Luxembourger	French/German/ Letzeburgish	Luxembourg
The Netherlands	Dutch	Dutchman/ -woman	Dutch	The Hague
Portugal	Portuguese	Portuguese	Portuguese	Lisbon
Spain	Spanish	Spaniard	Spanish	Madrid
Sweden	Swedish	Swede	Swedish	Stockholm
The United Kingdom	British	Briton	English	London

You may wish to introduce the vocabulary needed to describe regional variations, e.g. in Spain and the UK.

Spain	Catalonian Basque	Catalonian Basque	Spanish/Catalan Spanish/Basque	Barcelona Vitoria
United Kingdom				
· England	English	Englishman/ -woman	English	London
· Scotland	Scottish	Scotsman/ -woman	English/ Scottish Gaelic	Edinburgh
· Wales	Welsh	Welshman/ -woman	English/ Welsh	Cardiff
· Northern Ireland	Northern Irish	Northern Irishman/ -woman	English / Irish Gaelic	Belfast

Vocabulary check *119*

1. Financial support given by the Government or other organisation, e.g. to set up a business. *grant* or *subsidy*
2. To reserve a ticket. *book*
3. What you must pay for when your luggage is over the limit at the check-in at an airport. *excess luggage*
4. Another word for head office. *headquarters*
5. Another word for chance. *opportunity*
6. France is a net payer or *contributor* to the EU while Portugal is a net receiver or *recipient*.
7. Red tape means the same as *bureaucracy*.
8. Suitable or correct. *appropriate*

9. The abbreviation GDP stands for *Gross Domestic Product*.
10. An organisation's income. *revenue*

120 HAVING A GOOD TIME IN BRUSSELS

A. IN THE PUB

Please ask the students to refer to the Social English part of the Reference Section (pp. 289–294). When doing the Exercises 1 and 2 students should use the menu (p. 121).

▶ Note: In the poem on the menu the word *score* stands for *twenty.* In English-speaking countries the pub is an institution and there is a strong pub culture. People go not only to drink but to converse, to watch TV, to hold meetings. In the financial centres of London and Dublin you will find many businesspeople who frequent pubs to discuss business matters, to go for lunch and the traditional 'drink after work' with colleagues.

Students have to be made aware that going to the pub is seen as a normal part of business life. They should be prepared to participate in this traditional but important aspect of team-building which Continental Europeans sometimes underestimate. Negative aspects include not going to the pub with colleagues, not participating in conversations (forcing the other person(s) into monologues) and not understanding the system of buying drinks, i.e. the round system. Something as trivial as this can lead to embarrassing situations and very often damage business relations.

We strongly recommend practising role-play conversations in this area.

This could also be a good opportunity to discuss cultural differences (see also Unit 11).

122 B. MIXING FOOD WITH BUSINESS

lemon = C
nuts = H
baloney = F
peanuts = E

a piece of cake = B
a peach = I
in a pickle = A
the apple of his/her eye = J

fruitcake = L
to go bananas = K
fishy = G
to cream = D

C. AT A PARTY – ROLE-PLAYS

122 – 123

Here students have plenty of opportunities to role-play Social English. Please make sure that they vary their language by referring to Social Language in the Reference Section.

Simulation

123

This simulation is an extensive role-play where the students are expected to interchange roles. You should plan 30 to 40 minutes for this pair/group work activity. If there is more time available, students should contact several travel agents, hotels, etc for the best offer available. They could also role-play the first meeting/reception before the official start of the conference.

The restaurant scene could also take place in a real restaurant where students could meet for a drink and speak English. This underlines the importance of meeting with students in a more relaxed environment.

UNIT 8 RECRUITMENT

Story Line

Hazel already has her blue-collar workers signed up but urgently needs some office staff. For this reason she advertised in The Irish Times resulting in a number of applications for the positions of secretary and marketing assistant. John Elliott from Standard Irish Bank, still hooked on Hazel, helps her with the interviewing. For her new white-collar staff she employs Christian Birke for the marketing position and Sharon Steele as secretary.

Focus

- To advertise for staff
- To apply for a job
- To perform effectively in a job interview

▶ Note: Using the Internet links is especially important in this unit.

127 ADVERTISING FOR STAFF

This is a reading exercise followed by a comprehension check. As a follow-up exercise students could surf the Net for job vacancies and find out the requirements for a job that they would be interested in.

Although the Internet is increasingly used for job advertisements the whole recruitment procedure is still quite the same regardless of whether an application is sent by post or by e-mail. Job interviews by telephone are becoming more frequent, especially for lower-level positions.

129 Comprehension

1. In the classified section of the Irish Times.
2. Requirements for the marketing assistant: 2 years experience, proven track record, pro-active approach, flexibility.
   Requirements for the secretary: Candidate should be immediately available, have previous business experience, solid secretarial skills, excellent communication and spreadsheet skills, a pleasant personality, ability to prioritise work, speak foreign languages.
3. For the marketing assistant: An attractive salary, 25 days annual holiday, non-contributory pension scheme, an attractive work environment and genuine career progression.
   For the secretary: A competitive salary, good career prospects.
4. From Nelson and Son, where Hazel had done her placement.
5. A secretary and a marketing assistant for the start.
6. The company assesses the candidate and the candidate does the same with the company.

APPLICATIONS

131 – 132

A. CHRISTIAN BIRKE'S APPLICATION

On the following pages you find the completed application form. Students may have minor variations in their answers. Not all information required is provided in this personal story. Students, therefore, only fill in what is possible.

▶ Note: The *& YOU* as in CELTIC DESIGN JEWELLERY & YOU is quite commonly used on application forms.

Additional exercise:
Ask students to imagine that they are applying for a position in a company that they feel is relevant for their future. This can be based on a real ad from a Job Vacancies or Appointments page. For this exercise they should be provided with a copy of the blank application form (pp. 56–57). This is a useful writing exercise where time permits. Make sure students fill out form completing all details.

CELTIC DESIGN JEWELLERY & YOU

APPLICATION FORM

POSITION *Marketing Assistant*

PERSONAL DETAILS

SURNAME ***Birke*** FIRST NAME(S) ***Christian***

DATE OF BIRTH ***March 30, 1974***

ADDRESS ***41 Kingston Road, Rathmines, Dublin 6***

TELEPHONE; FAX; E-MAIL ***8766532 (home telephone only)***

MARITAL STATUS ***Single/Unmarried***

CHILDREN ***(not stated)***

131 – 132 **ACADEMIC HISTORY**
(PLEASE INCLUDE DATES, NAMES AND LOCATIONS)

SECONDARY EDUCATION ***Gorlitz Secondary School 1986 - 1992***
Chemnitz, Free State of Saxony
HIGHER EDUCATION ***Dresden University of Technology***

MAJOR EXAMINATION ***German School Leaving Certificate 1992***
RESULTS ***MA in Business Administration (specialising in Marketing, Accounting and Finance, Tourism Administration and English) 1992-1997***
TRAINING (COURSES ATTENDED/ QUALIFICATIONS OBTAINED) ***European Marketing Course***
Webster's Graduate Studies Centre Regent St London, United Kingdom
ADDITIONAL SKILLS ***MS-Windows, MS-Excel, MS-Word***
SPSS (Graphics program for Market Research)
Do you have a current driving licence? ***(Presume answer is Yes)***

Are you willing to travel? ***(Presume answer is Yes)***

WORK EXPERIENCE

PRESENT POST (TITLE, LENGTH OF SERVICE, CURRENT SALARY) ***Currently between jobs***

PREVIOUS POSTS HELD (INCLUDING PART-TIME OR HOLIDAY JOBS)

EMPLOYER	JOB TITLE	DATES	REASONS FOR LEAVING
Henkel Home Improvements & Adhesive Products, Dresden and London	***Marketing Ass.***	***1993-1997***	***not stated***
SKR Advertising Agency, Manchester		***1997-2000***	***Irish girlfriend***

LANGUAGE AND TRAVEL Please give brief details of residence or recent travel abroad, if any.
Resident in UK and Republic of Ireland

Please state degree of fluency in any foreign language
German (mother tongue) French (basic)
English (fluent) Russian (basic)

INTERESTS AND HOBBIES
Am interested in travelling, hiking, music, movies and computers.

REFEREES (one from current or previous employer, one from personal referee)
1. Ms Janet Long, Manager
SKR Advertisement Agency,
Manchester, United Kingdom

2. Prof. Michael Schmidt,
Faculty of Economics
Dresden University of Technology, Germany

WHAT ATTRACTS YOU TO THIS POST? 131 – 132
I see good opportunities in a firm this size and would enjoy the challenge of helping it develop its potential.

HOW DO YOU THINK YOU CAN CONTRIBUTE TO THIS POST?
I have gained a lot of experience particularly in the marketing area in both Germany and the UK which could prove very useful for Celtic Design Jewellery.

WHAT HAS GIVEN YOU THE GREATEST SATISFACTION TO DATE IN YOUR CURRENT OR PREVIOUS EMPLOYMENT?
The production of the £1m TV commercial involved a lot of hard work but the end result was really satisfying.

BRIEFLY EXPLAIN HOW YOU SEE YOUR CAREER DEVELOPING OVER THE NEXT FIVE YEARS
That's difficult to answer. I can say that I would like to see it progress as the company progresses.

HOW SOON COULD YOU START WORK IF APPOINTED?
Immediately, as I do not have to give any notice.

ANY FURTHER INFORMATION YOU WOULD LIKE TO ADD IN SUPPORT OF YOUR APPLICATION?
I would prefer to wait and explain all at the interview.

SIGNED *Christian Birke* DATE *July 24 20..*

____________ & YOU

APPLICATION FORM

POSITION

PERSONAL DETAILS

SURNAME FIRST NAME(S)

DATE OF BIRTH

ADDRESS

TELEPHONE; FAX; E-MAIL

MARITAL STATUS

CHILDREN

ACADEMIC HISTORY
(PLEASE INCLUDE DATES, NAMES AND LOCATIONS)

SECONDARY EDUCATION

HIGHER EDUCATION

MAJOR EXAMINATION
RESULTS

TRAINING (COURSES ATTENDED/
QUALIFICATIONS OBTAINED)

ADDITIONAL SKILLS

Do you have a current
driving licence?

Are you willing to travel?

WORK EXPERIENCE

PRESENT POST (TITLE, LENGTH OF SERVICE, CURRENT SALARY)

PREVIOUS POSTS HELD (INCLUDING PART-TIME OR HOLIDAY JOBS)

EMPLOYER	JOB TITLE	DATES	REASONS FOR LEAVING

LANGUAGE AND TRAVEL Please give brief details of residence or recent travel abroad, if any.

Please state degree of fluency in any foreign language

INTERESTS AND HOBBIES

REFEREES (one from current or previous employer, one from personal referee)

WHAT ATTRACTS YOU TO THIS POST?

HOW DO YOU THINK YOU CAN CONTRIBUTE TO THIS POST?

WHAT HAS GIVEN YOU THE GREATEST SATISFACTION TO DATE IN YOUR CURRENT OR PREVIOUS EMPLOYMENT?

BRIEFLY EXPLAIN HOW YOU SEE YOUR CAREER DEVELOPING OVER THE NEXT FIVE YEARS

HOW SOON COULD YOU START WORK IF APPOINTED?

ANY FURTHER INFORMATION YOU WOULD LIKE TO ADD IN SUPPORT OF YOUR APPLICATION?

SIGNED DATE

133 – 134 **B. SHARON STEELE'S RESUMÉ AND LETTER OF APPLICATION**

1. Compare Sharon's resumé with Hazel's CV in Unit 1 (p. 6). Refer to the Reference Section, p. 270. If a CV/resumé was not attempted in Unit 1, now is a good time. The students may also want to update their old one(s).

2. It may be useful to point out differences between BE and AE concerning writing. See Date, Salutation and Complimentary Close under Layout of Letters (pp. 272–274). You will also find the EU directive on writing (p. 272). For letters of application please refer the students to pp. 276–277.

   Instructors should also be aware that there is an exercise in Unit 11 (p. 209) on differences between American and British English words.

   Sample Solution: position – advertized (AE)
   firm/company – opportunity (chance is too informal) – qualities
   travels – absence
   interview – resumé/CV – information – contact – brochure – advance/anticipation.

   ▶ Note: In BE 's' is used (as in *organisation*), in AE 'z' is preferred (*organization*).

135 **Writing Practice**

For exercises 1 and 2 please refer to pp. 276–277. Exercise 1 can be based on a real ad from a Job Vacancies or Appointments page.

▶ Note: The date on a *printed letterhead* can be either on the left-hand side of the page (see p. 273) or on the right-hand side. On *other types* of letters the date is often written below the sender's address on the right-hand side. There should be at least a one-line space between the address and the date (see sample letter p. 134).

INTERVIEWING

Make students aware of the Interview Checklist in the Job Interview part of the Reference Section (pp. 281–282). As a lead-in ask your students to discuss their own experience with job interviews, if they have any. They could focus on questions asked, interviewing climate, tests, etc. Alternatively, you can discuss this as a follow-up exercise after listening to Sharon Steele's interview (p. 143).

Ask students to read through the introduction (p. 135) before filling in the interview guide sheet.

A. INTERVIEW GUIDE SHEET

136

INTERVIEW GUIDE SHEET

1. B*e* prepared. Ha*ve* all candidate information available. Arr*ange* appropriate interview room and org*anise* table, chairs, etc accordingly. En*sure* that there will be no interruptions during interview, e.g. ma*ke* certain phone is off the hook. Pl*an* how you are going to conduct interview.

2. Wel*come* candidate. Gr*eet* candidate and th*ank* them for coming. Int*roduce* yourself and re*lax* candidate. St*art* interview by asking mild questions, gradually building up the tempo. Vary interview using open-ended and closed questions.

3. Gi*ve* candidate opportunity to talk and express ideas but make sure you control the interview.

4. Al*low* the candidate a question time.

5. Cl*lose* interview. In*form* candidate of next step. Thank candidate for responses to questions. S*ay* goodbye.

6. Wr*ite* up notes and ex*press* views on candidate.

7. D*o* final evaluation at end of interviewing.

137 – 138 **B. SHARON STEELE'S INTERVIEW**

1. ▶ Note: If you have time constraints it is not necessary to go through the two interviews presented in this unit. A lot of relevant interview language is covered in both of them. Depending on your group you may prefer to work on the secretary (Sharon Steele) or the marketing assistant interview (Christian Birke).

H: Come in please, Sharon Steele ... this is Mr Elliott, he will be conducting the interview with me.
Mr E: How do you do?
Ms S: *How do you do?*
H: Have a seat please, Ms Steele.
Ms S: Thank you.
Mr E: I trust you had no problem in finding the place.
Ms S: *No, not at all* .
H: You have an interesting CV. Now, I wonder, can you tell me what type of person you are?
Ms S: Well, *I would describe myself* as serious-minded ... calm.
H: Calm?
Ms S: Yes. *I can work well under pressure.*
H: Why have you decided to apply for a position with us?
Ms S: Well, *I feel like a change* . I was just looking around really ... but I was really impressed with your company leaflet ... it's something new. I'm a secretary ... a trained secretary, but in my current job ... I feel, well, ... that I'm going nowhere fast. I never had the chance to go on to university ... A degree isn't everything ... but people expect you to have it if you want to get on. I feel that given the chance I can really show what I've got. To be honest, if I get this job, I hope to be more than a secretary in the future.
H: Oh yeah ... I also think a degree is not so special. Anyhow, *where do you see yourself* in five years' time?
Ms S: Well, ... assuming that the company develops, I'd like to see myself getting into the management side of things. I'm prepared to do a relevant evening course.
H: Do you intend having a family in the next three years?
Ms S: *I haven't thought much about that* actually. I think I've still got enough time.
H: So you've got no problem with doing a lot of overtime if the need arises?
Ms S: No.
Mr E: Why do you feel you're getting nowhere in your current job?
Ms S: Well, it's the manager ...
Mr E: What do you mean?

Ms S: Well, it seems as *if the right hand doesn't know what the left hand is doing*. The internal communications should be a lot better ... by letting people know what's going on rather than letting them find out for themselves. We seem to be moving from one crisis to another. There seems to be no staff development plan, no annual assessment ...

Mr E: What exactly do you do in the company?

Ms S: Different things – answering the phone, correspondence, doing the typing, filing. I've done reception for five weeks and organised some work projects *– the work really isn't challenging*. I'd like more scope.

Mr E: What, for example?

Ms S: Well ... working on projects where you need to use your brains a bit more than at present, like setting up meetings, doing a company presentation — even to travel. *Not the same hum-drum routine* secretarial-work every day.

H: I see that you did French and Spanish at school. How good are you in everyday communication in these languages?

Ms S: Well ... you've got my resumé. What it doesn't say is that my favourite subject was French *and I've kept it up*. I actually went to France as an au-pair for three months. I guess I should have mentioned that. My Spanish is a bit rusty, I'm afraid ...

(*The same interview nearing its conclusion a few minutes later.*)

H: I see. Em ... Ms Steele ... one final question, why should we give you the job?

Ms S: Well, it may sound arrogant and ... I've got no real references to back me up ... but I feel that *I've got a lot to offer*. My boss knows it ... that's why I'm not sure he would give me a reference. I didn't ask. As I said earlier, I feel that I'm really good at working with people, I can talk to strangers, *I'm able to work on my own*. I can deal with the difficult customers.

Mr E: Have you any questions for us?

Ms S: Yes, I have ... I mean, if I get the job *will you reward good work*, will I be able to get on?

H: It all depends on how we do ... but ... yeah ... I can promise you that.

Ms S: *How long is the probation period* ?

H: Six months. That's the usual.

Ms S: Fine, I think that's all.

Mr E: Ms Steele, thank you very much for coming along. *You'll hear from us in a week or so.*

Ms S: OK, thank you very much. Goodbye.

H: You're welcome.

Mr E: Goodbye.

139 Comprehension/Discussion

1. Students should attempt to do this exercise from memory. Afterwards, they could go through the transcript for more complete answers or alternatively listen to this interview again.

   A. She describes herself as calm, serious-minded, able to work under pressure.
   B. She feels like a change, was impressed by the company leaflet, is looking for a more challenging position.
   C. She hopes to be more than a secretary in the future, would like to be involved in managing the business and is prepared to do relevant evening courses.
   D. She is willing to work overtime if the need arises.
   E. She describes her present employer as badly organised, crisis-prone, with no staff development plan, no staff evaluation.
   F. It involves answering the phone, correspondence, typing, filing, doing reception, occasionally also the organisation of work projects.
   G. She speaks Spanish (although it's a bit rusty), and French (fluently).
   H. In her opinion she has got a lot to offer, she is good at working with people, she has no problems with strangers and difficult customers and is able to work on her own.

2. The students may come up with different responses. Her open criticism of her current manager may make a negative impression.

3. Let the students listen to the interviewers' analysis of Sharon and compare it with their own opinions.

140 C. INTERVIEW WITH CHRISTIAN BIRKE

This is another listening exercise requiring students to keep their books closed. The eight points should be put on the board/OHP or dictated before commencing the exercise.

C. studies
B. previous work experience
G. reasons for changing employer in the past
D. reasons for applying for the job
H. candidate's ideas for the job offered
F. plans for the future
A. perks
E. further training

Optional exercise 142

This is taken from the Job Interview part of the Reference Section. It is a good exercise for students to use the phrases needed to express themselves clearly in this particular situation. The students may refer to a job advertisement that is relevant for them to make it more realistic.

Possible answers for Christian Birke:
(Details of Sharon Steele's interview have already been discussed, p. 139)

A: ... it's a real challenge. I believe, I'm a good team worker, I have good computer skills, I speak foreign languages. This company is small, I think I can help it grow.
B: What your company is trying is really interesting. (He also makes proposals for a marketing strategy for Hazel's business.)
C: – Not mentioned in the interview. (Please refer to "A Life", course book, p. 130, which is the basis for completing the application form, pp. 131-32. There Christian mentions travelling and computers.)
D: I believe I'm a good team worker, I have good computer skills, I speak foreign languages.
E: Christian refers to his degree and main subjects and his experience in marketing and advertising and asks about training for the job he is applying for.

EVALUATING

Name	Strengths	Weaknesses
Stewart	Experience, good personality	Appearance
Sweeney	Smart appearance, experience, contacts	No driving license, bad reference
Birke	Answered well, experience, marketing knowledge	Slight German accent

Discussion/Role-play 143

Discussing these aspects of job interviews and giving the students an opportunity to practise an interview situation is highly recommendable as practically all of them will face such a situation at one stage or another in their life. Exercise 5 can be done as homework.

144 **Vocabulary check**

1. A more formal word for job vacancies. *appointments*
2. Needed. *required*
3. Pension paid for by the employer. *non-contributory pension*
4. Section in the paper where you could find cars for sale. *classifieds*
5. A more noticeable and more expensive newspaper advertisement. *display*
6. Person applying for a job. *applicant*
7. Another name for employee evaluation. *staff assessment*
8. The time off when you are ill. *sick-leave*
9. American word for CV. *resumé*
10. Formal announcement of intention to end employment. *notice*
11. A person who really wants to climb the career ladder is said to be *ambitious*.
12. Another name for severance pay. *redundancy payment*
13. A person who works on the shop floor. *blue-collar employee*
14. To hire is to *employ*.
15. Additional material benefits from a job. *fringe benefits/perks*
16. What one pays into for one's retirement. *pension scheme/plan*

Simulation

Here students have to recruit suitable staff for their own business.

Suggested approach:
It is a good idea to have two groups that work together. The members of each team apply for a job offered by the other team/firm.

This is a more extensive simulation where the groups first decide on the vacant position(s) for their business (one or two will do), and afterwards draft the ad(s) which the students of the other group get to read (copies should be prepared beforehand!). As homework, each student has to write a CV and letter of application for (one of) the position(s) offered by the partner group. In the following period the teams get together, read the applications from the members of the other group and plan the interviews. Then the interviewing starts. At the end the most suitable candidate for each position has to be found.

Story Line

Hazel goes about getting insurance cover for her business. Ray Connors, a friend of hers in the insurance business, fills her in as she's not too well-informed about this particular area.

Focus

- To provide an understanding of the fundamentals of insurance as required by the average businessperson
- To enable students to fill in a standard proposal form in English
- To review telephoning in an insurance context

TELEPHONING AN INSURANCE OFFICE *149*

Students do the listening activity.

Memo

First name:	Ray Connors
Surname:	Hibernia Insurance Company Claims department
Company's name:	257 secretary's name is Julia
Department:	Hazel's friend, has a hangover Thursday, 10 o' clock
Extension number:	Business Compact proposal form

THE INSURANCE PROPOSAL FORM *150*

This section will provide your students with basic concepts and terminology connected with insurance. The proposal form format has been chosen to make it as realistic as possible.

▶ Note: When filling the form certain parts or sections may not be pertinent or relevant. In this case, the abbreviation *n/a, not applicable*, should be used. The abbreviation *T/A* stands for *trading as.*

Additional information for instructors is contained in brackets on the form below.

√ stands for *tick*.

Students ***x*** or cross the boxes.

Inform students that the postal address can be her private or business one.

The *For Office Use Only* section does not have to be filled in!

BUSINESS COMPACT INSURANCE

INSURANCE PROTECTION FOR YOUR BUSINESS

PROPOSAL

PLEASE ANSWER ALL QUESTIONS IN BLOCK CAPITALS

150 NAME OF PROPOSER AND BUSINESS IN FULL

HAZEL NORA BROWNE T/A CELTIC DESIGN JEWELLERY LTD

POSTAL ADDRESS

54 COLLINS AVENUE, WHITEHALL, DUBLIN 3

BUSINESS OR OCCUPATION (IF MORE THAN ONE, STATE ALL)

JEWELLERY MANUFACTURER

SITUATION OF PROPERTY TO BE INSURED (IF DIFFERENT FROM POSTAL ADDRESS)

SUMMERHILL ESTATE, DUBLIN 24

FOR OFFICE USE ONLY

PERIOD OF INSURANCE FROM TO

RENEWAL DATE

BRANCH BRANCH CODE

AGENCY (PLEASE QUOTE AGENCY NO.)

POLICY NUMBER

HIBERNIA

A word from the Insurance Institute of the United Kingdom and Ireland

We've come a long way since the modern system of insurance first started hundreds of years ago in Edward Lloyd's coffee shop. In the modern world the importance of insurance is often taken for granted despite it being a major employment sector and of vital importance to any modern economy.

Insurance
- helps to relieve business people from some of the risks they face and thereby encourages them to take part in enterprises resulting in much increased economic activity.
- is a huge invisible export with profits from overseas transactions having a very positive effect on the balance of payments of our two countries. Can we even start to imagine where foreign trade would be without aviation or marine insurance?
- offers on an individual level (life cover) not only personal protection but also serves as an investment opportunity for millions of people.

INSURANCE – Serving YOUR Needs Today!

<u>GLOSSARY</u>
Insurance – provision made for any loss or damage to person, property or business. The two parties to an insurance contract are referred to as the *insurance company* or *insurer* and the person requiring cover, known as the insured.
There are five main classes: FIRE (standard fire cover plus special perils, household cover), ACCIDENT (motor, personal accident, illness, burglary, fidelity guarantee and liability), LIFE, MARINE, ENGINEERING and AVIATION.

Policy – the written contract between the two parties.
Premium – fee charged by the insurer for providing cover.
Proposal – printed document where individual (or broker) makes a written application for the issue of the policy.

MAIN PRINCIPLES OF INSURANCE

- **Insurable Interest** – The insured must have an insurable interest in the object insured, i.e. property, rights, interest, life or limb, etc. One must benefit by the existence of the object and suffer by its loss.
- **Utmost Good Faith** – The person seeking insurance must disclose all relevant information. Non-disclosure can render the insurance contract void.
- **Indemnity** – The insurer will indemnify the insured to the extent of any loss suffered but the insured will never be placed in a better position than before the loss occured, i.e. the insured cannot recover a sum greater than the loss sustained. Life assurance is regarded as an exception.

SECTION 1
FIRE, SPECIAL PERILS, BURGLARY AND HOLD UP
(N.B. PLEASE TICK APPROPRIATELY)

Is Fire section required? ☑ YES ☐ NO
(NOTE: Also includes damage caused in extinguishing fire)

Select contingencies in addition to Fire

Burglary and Hold Up	☑ YES	☐ NO	Earthquake	☐ YES	☑ NO
Burst Pipes	☑ YES	☐ NO	Storm and Flood	☐ YES	☑ NO
Riots/Malicious Damage	☐ YES	☑ NO	Impact	☐ YES	☑ NO

(NOTE: There is a € 200 excess on each and every loss)

PROPERTY TO BE INSURED

SUMS TO BE INSURED

	Fire & Special Perils	Burglary and Hold Up
1. Building including fixtures and fittings	*€ 250K*	*€ 250K*
2. Stock and materials	*€ 30K*	*€ 30K*
TOTAL SUM INSURED	*€ 280K*	*€ 280K*

A. CONSTRUCTION Are the buildings all constructed of standard materials?
☑ YES ☐ NO If No, give details.

B. HEIGHT How many storeys are there over basement? One

C. UNOCCUPANCY To what extent will your premises be left unoccupied?
☐ By day ☑ By night

D. SECURITY
Are all external doors, windows and other openings secured and the intruder alarm (if any) 'set' when premises are closed? ☑ YES ☐ NO

Are premises supervised by a security firm/caretaker etc?
☐ YES ☑ NO

→

SECTION 2
BUSINESS INTERRUPTION/CONSEQUENTIAL LOSS

Is this section required? ☑ YES ☐ NO
(NOTE: This covers loss of profits following fire and any other perils covered.)

What sum insured do you require? *(students decide)*

SECTION 3
LOSS OF MONEY & ASSAULT

Is this section required? ☐ YES ☑ NO
What is the annual limit of indemnity required? *n/a*
What does it comprise (cash, cheques etc)? *n/a*

How is it secured in:
a) the premises? ☐ By day ☐ By night
b) in transit? *n/a*

(NOTE: **Fidelity Guarantee** cover against fraud and theft by employees is also available – please ask for details.) 150

SECTION 4
LIABILITY INSURANCE

Is this section required? ☑ YES ☐ NO
EMPLOYER'S LIABILITY (Death/injury to employees in course of employment)? ☑ YES ☐ NO
PUBLIC LIABILITY (Death/injury to members of public on premises of insured)? ☑ YES ☐ NO
PRODUCT'S LIABILITY (NOTE: Various covers available – please ask for details)? ☑ YES ☐ NO

1. Describe precisely:
a) Work undertaken *firm designs and manufactures Celtic jewellery*

b) Goods supplied, installed, erected, repaired, altered, etc.
(Please attach copies of all catalogues, brochures or other literature)
n/a

2. Have you any other liability insurance? ☐ YES ☑ NO
(Hazel's TPFT is motor insurance rather than liability.)
3. Do you export outside the Republic of Ireland? ☑ YES ☐ NO
(If yes, give full particulars.) *EU*

4. Do you import goods, materials, parts etc from outside the EU?
☐ YES ☑ NO
5. Do you issue any written guarantees? ☑ YES ☐ NO
(If yes, please attach specimen.)
6. Have you prepared written safety guidelines according to the Safety at Work Act, 1989?
☑ YES ☐ NO

SCHEDULE OF EMPLOYEES

Description of Work	No. of Employees	Wages/Salaries
1. Clerical and non-manual	*3*	*€ 45K*
2. Machinists		
3. All other employees	*3*	*€ 40K*
4. All other persons who enter premises		

SECTION 5
MACHINES AND EQUIPMENT

Is this section required? ☑ YES ☐ NO
(NOTE: Covers loss or damage by fire, theft or accidental means of machines or pieces of equipment on the premises, with an option of wider cover)

DESCRIPTION OF MACHINES OR EQUIPMENT

ITEM 1 *Black & Decker 921 Multi-Purpose, 1999 Model*

SUM TO BE INSURED *€ 3,800*

ITEM 2 *Cordon 54 Cutter, 1999 Model*

SUM TO BE INSURED *€ 5000*

SECTION 6
MOTOR FLEET

1. Are you the legal owner of the vehicle(s)? ☑ YES ☐ NO
2. In whose name are the vehicle(s) registered? *Hazel Nora Browne*
3. How and where are the vehicle(s) usually safeguarded overnight?
Vehicles kept overnight in secured company garage

→

4. Total number of vehicle(s) of all classes owned by proposer 2
   (only concerned with Motor Fleet of company)

5. Please give particulars of all purposes for which the vehicle(s) will be used.
   Transport of raw materials and finished goods.

6. If used for carriage of goods, will any goods be of an explosive, corrosive, radioactive or other hazardous nature? ☐ YES ☑ NO

Motor Fleet Schedule

- Please supply a printed schedule including name, date of birth, occupation and driving licence of all drivers to be covered. A detailed medical certificate stating current state of health must be submitted. Full particulars of prosecutions or prosecutions pending are also required.
- A printed list of all vehicles stating registration no, make and model, cc, year of manufacture, value and years of N.C.B.

7. Indicate cover required:	**No. of**	**T.P.**[1]	**T.P.F.T.**[2]	**Comp.**[3]	150
Cars	1		✓		
Commercial Vehicles (vans etc)	1		✓		
Tractors and Special Types	n/a				

NOTE:

1) T.P. (Third Party) = the minimum insurance required by any motorist who wants to drive a vehicle on the road so that in the event of an accident the other motorist, i.e. the third party, is covered for any injuries received and any damage to his/her vehicle.
2) T.P.F.T. (Third Party, Fire and Theft) = covers the insured for loss or damage caused by fire and loss due to theft in addition to T.P. cover.
3) Comp. = Comprehensive or Full Cover where all parties and vehicles are fully insured.

If entitled to No Claims Bonus (N.C.B.) please supply written proof of number of years entitlement.

157 **Vocabulary check**

Make sure that the students read the definitions (pp. 152-53) before attempting this exercise.

1. *Fidelity Guarantee* is especially useful where employees are entrusted with the handling of money, e.g. cashiers, accountants.
2. An employee who loses a hand or finger operating a machine is entitled to compensation under *Employer's Liability*.
3. A young girl who slips at a disco on a wet floor and breaks a leg is covered under *Public Liability*.
4. *Fire* insurance also includes damage caused by water used to put out a fire.
5. It is also possible to be covered against loss of profits or other income while the business premises are being repaired or rebuilt. This is referred to as *Business Interruption/ Consequential Loss*.
6. While speeding you crash into another motorist. Repair costs to your damaged car are only covered if you have *Comprehensive/Full Cover* insurance.

157 GETTING INSURANCE ADVICE

This is another listening exercise requiring the students to keep their books closed.

▶ Note: *re* p. 158: The Federal Reserve (Fed) is the U.S. Central Bank.

1. Quotations are not his business, he works in the claims department.
2. Hazel should go to the customer's service and ask Louise to help her. She should also contact other insurance brokers to get the best quotation and should not forget to read the small print.
3. Get quotations from different insurers, decide on the best, fill out a proposal form, hand it in. Then the insurance company will send you the policy.
4. *Whole life insurance* means that a premium is paid for one's whole life and the beneficiaries stated in the policy receive a lump sum after your death. *Endowment* is an arrangement where the premiums are paid for an agreed number of years and the sum assured is paid either as a lump sum or on a regular basis at the end of this period or after the death of the insured.
5. Insurance is something that might happen, whereas assurance is something that will definitely happen.

Vocabulary check
159 – 160

1. This exercise is primarily intended as homework after the first part of the unit has been done.

A. protecting/insuring/indemnifying
B. insurer/insurance company
C. insured
D. insurable interest
E. Indemnity
F. utmost good faith
G. policy
H. premium
I. claim
J. settle
K. insurance
L. assurance
M. Whole life
N. Endowment
O. employer's, public
P. third party, comprehensive
Q. renewal form

2.
160

to protect against – a risk/a loss
to complete – a proposal form/a claim form
to insure – a person's life/a risk
to fill in – a claim form/a proposal form
to pay – a claim /a lump sum
to cover – a risk/a person's life
to file – a claim
to provide – cover/compensation
to cover against – a loss/a risk
to take out – a policy
to suffer – a loss/damage
to settle – a claim

Discussion
161

1. Mr Hodges is over-insured, so he only receives the current market value of the house. (Principle of Indemnity)
2. False information was given, so the insurance contract is null and void. The claim is rejected by the insurance company on this basis. (Principle of Utmost Good Faith)
3. The claim for theft and damage to apartment is approved. (Covered under the Household Policy)
4. The insurance policy is null and void as renewal wasn't paid. The claim is rejected. The employee must take legal action against the employer as the employer failed to renew the policy as per his/her legal obligation.
5. This is an identical situation to No. 2.

Role-play
162 – 163

These are guided role-plays for students to practice telephoning in an insurance context.

Simulation
163

As insurance is a challenging topic for most students, the simulation provides another opportunity to consolidate. Instructors should provide copies of the Business Compact proposal form as it helps the course participants to get to grips with the terminology.

BUSINESS COMPACT INSURANCE

INSURANCE PROTECTION FOR YOUR BUSINESS

PROPOSAL

PLEASE ANSWER ALL QUESTIONS IN BLOCK CAPITALS

NAME OF PROPOSER AND BUSINESS IN FULL

POSTAL ADDRESS

BUSINESS OR OCCUPATION (IF MORE THAN ONE, STATE ALL)

SITUATION OF PROPERTY TO BE INSURED (IF DIFFERENT FROM POSTAL ADDRESS)

FOR OFFICE USE ONLY

PERIOD OF INSURANCE FROM TO

RENEWAL DATE

BRANCH BRANCH CODE

AGENCY (PLEASE QUOTE AGENCY NO.)

POLICY NUMBER

HIBERNIA

A word from the Insurance Institute of the United Kingdom and Ireland

We've come a long way since the modern system of insurance first started hundreds of years ago in Edward Lloyd's coffee shop. In the modern world the importance of insurance is often taken for granted despite it being a major employment sector and of vital importance to any modern economy.

Insurance

- helps to relieve business people from some of the risks they face and thereby encourages them to take part in enterprises resulting in much increased economic activity.
- is a huge invisible export with profits from overseas transactions having a very positive effect on the balance of payments of our two countries. Can we even start to imagine where foreign trade would be without aviation or marine insurance?
- offers on an individual level (life cover) not only personal protection but also serves as an investment opportunity for millions of people.

INSURANCE – Serving YOUR Needs Today!

GLOSSARY

Insurance – provision made for any loss or damage to person, property or business. The two parties to an insurance contract are referred to as the *insurance company* or *insurer* and the person requiring cover, known as the insured.
There are five main classes: FIRE (standard fire cover plus special perils, household cover), ACCIDENT (motor, personal accident, illness, burglary, fidelity guarantee and liability), LIFE, MARINE, ENGINEERING and AVIATION.

Policy – the written contract between the two parties.
Premium – fee charged by the insurer for providing cover.
Proposal – printed document where individual (or broker) makes a written application for the issue of the policy.

MAIN PRINCIPLES OF INSURANCE

- **Insurable Interest** – The insured must have an insurable interest in the object insured, i.e. property, rights, interest, life or limb, etc. One must benefit by the existence of the object and suffer by its loss.
- **Utmost Good Faith** – The person seeking insurance must disclose all relevant information. Non-disclosure can render the insurance contract void.
- **Indemnity** – The insurer will indemnify the insured to the extent of any loss suffered but the insured will never be placed in a better position than before the loss occured, i.e. the insured cannot recover a sum greater than the loss sustained. Life assurance is regarded as an exception.

SECTION 1
FIRE, SPECIAL PERILS, BURGLARY AND HOLD UP
(N.B. PLEASE TICK APPROPRIATELY)

Is Fire section required? ☐ YES ☐ NO
(NOTE: Also includes damage caused in extinguishing fire)

Select contingencies in addition to Fire

Burglary and Hold Up	☐ YES	☐ NO	Earthquake	☐ YES	☐ NO
Burst Pipes	☐ YES	☐ NO	Storm and Flood	☐ YES	☐ NO
Riots/Malicious Damage	☐ YES	☐ NO	Impact	☐ YES	☐ NO

(NOTE: There is a € 200 excess on each and every loss)

PROPERTY TO BE INSURED

SUMS TO BE INSURED

	Fire & Special Perils	**Burglary and Hold Up**
1. Building including fixtures and fittings		
2. Stock and materials		
TOTAL SUM INSURED		

A. CONSTRUCTION Are the buildings all constructed of standard materials?
☐ YES ☐ NO If No, give details.

B. HEIGHT How many storeys are there over basement?

C. UNOCCUPANCY To what extent will your premises be left unoccupied?
☐ By day ☐ By night

D. SECURITY
Are all external doors, windows and other openings secured and the intruder alarm (if any) 'set' when premises are closed? ☐ YES ☐ NO

Are premises supervised by a security firm/caretaker etc?
☐ YES ☐ NO

→

SECTION 2
BUSINESS INTERRUPTION/CONSEQUENTIAL LOSS

Is this section required? ☐ YES ☐ NO
(NOTE: This covers loss of profits following fire and any other perils covered.)

What sum insured do you require? ______________________

SECTION 3
LOSS OF MONEY & ASSAULT

Is this section required? ☐ YES ☐ NO
What is the annual limit of indemnity required? ______________________
What does it comprise (cash, cheques etc)? ______________________

How is it secured in:
a) the premises? ☐ By day ☐ By night
b) in transit? ______________________

(NOTE: **Fidelity Guarantee** cover against fraud and theft by employees is also available – please ask for details.)

SECTION 4
LIABILITY INSURANCE

Is this section required? ☐ YES ☐ NO
EMPLOYER'S LIABILITY (Death/injury to employees in course of employment)?
☐ YES ☐ NO
PUBLIC LIABILITY (Death/injury to members of public on premises of insured)?
☐ YES ☐ NO
PRODUCT'S LIABILITY (NOTE: Various covers available – please ask for details)?
☐ YES ☐ NO

1. Describe precisely:
a) Work undertaken ______________________
____

b) Goods supplied, installed, erected, repaired, altered, etc.
(Please attach copies of all catalogues, brochures or other literature)
____

2. Have you any other liability insurance? ☐ YES ☐ NO
3. Do you export outside the Republic of Ireland? ☐ YES ☐ NO
(If yes, give full particulars.)

4. Do you import goods, materials, parts etc from outside the EU?
☐ YES ☐ NO
5. Do you issue any written guarantees? ☐ YES ☐ NO
(If yes, please attach specimen.)
6. Have you prepared written safety guidelines according to the Safety at Work Act, 1989?
☐ YES ☐ NO

SCHEDULE OF EMPLOYEES

Description of Work	No. of Employees	Wages/Salaries
1. Clerical and non-manual		
2. Machinists		
3. All other employees		
4. All other persons who enter premises		

SECTION 5
MACHINES AND EQUIPMENT

Is this section required? ☐ YES ☐ NO
(NOTE: Covers loss or damage by fire, theft or accidental means of machines or pieces of equipment on the premises, with an option of wider cover)

DESCRIPTION OF MACHINES OR EQUIPMENT ______________________
ITEM 1 ______________________
____
SUM TO BE INSURED ______________________
ITEM 2 ______________________
____
SUM TO BE INSURED ______________________

SECTION 6
MOTOR FLEET

1. Are you the legal owner of the vehicle(s)? ☐ YES ☐ NO
2. In whose name are the vehicle(s) registered? ______________________
3. How and where are the vehicle(s) usually safeguarded overnight? ______________________
____

→

4. Total number of vehicle(s) of all classes owned by proposer ________________

5. Please give particulars of all purposes for which the vehicle(s) will be used.
____

6. If used for carriage of goods, will any goods be of an explosive, corrosive, radioactive or other hazardous nature? ☐ YES ☐ NO

Motor Fleet Schedule

- Please supply a printed schedule including name, date of birth, occupation and driving licence of all drivers to be covered. A detailed medical certificate stating current state of health must be submitted. Full particulars of prosecutions or prosecutions pending are also required.
- A printed list of all vehicles stating registration no, make and model, cc, year of manufacture, value and years of N.C.B.

7. Indicate cover required:	**No. of**	**T.P.**[1]	**T.P.F.T.**[2]	**Comp.**[3]
Cars				
Commercial Vehicles (vans etc)				
Tractors and Special Types				

NOTE:

1) T.P. (Third Party) = the minimum insurance required by any motorist who wants to drive a vehicle on the road so that in the event of an accident the other motorist, i.e. the third party, is covered for any injuries received and any damage to his/her vehicle.
2) T.P.F.T. (Third Party, Fire and Theft) = covers the insured for loss or damage caused by fire and loss due to theft in addition to T.P. cover.
3) Comp. = Comprehensive or Full Cover where all parties and vehicles are fully insured.

If entitled to No Claims Bonus (N.C.B.) please supply written proof of number of years entitlement.

Story Line

The relationship between Hazel and John Elliott is over. Martin, a university student, has been taken on by the company for the summer. Christian is responsible for training him in. Like in all firms there's a lot of correspondence that has to be dealt with.

Focus

- To introduce commercial terminology, i.e. business documents, terms of payment and delivery (INCOTERMS), export documentation
- To practise commercial correspondence, i.e. enquiry, offer, order, and invoice

General note: It is necessary that the students should familiarise themselves with the respective Letter Writing part of the Reference Section (pp. 271–280) before attempting any of the letter-writing activities. The date on a *printed letterhead* can be either on the left-hand side of the page (see sample, p. 273) or alternatively on the right-hand side. On *other types of letters* the date is often written below the sender's address on the right-hand side. There should be at least a one-line space between the address and the date (see sample, p. 134).

BUSINESS DOCUMENTS

169 Ask students to familiarise themselves with the memo format which also sets the scene for the unit (see also Reference Section, p. 280).

170 **Social English**

If necessary, the students may refer to Making Contact (p. 289) in the Reference Section before doing the role-play.

170 – 171 **A–Z of Business Documents**

Here the students get an overview of a business transaction chain from the enquiry onwards. They should go through the list of business documents (pp. 171–172) before attempting the gap-filling exercise and, finally, listen to the cassette/CD to check answers.

"So, Martin, I'll make it as short as I can. First of all, potential customers usually send in a *letter of enquiry* and we reply with an *offer*. This could be a *catalogue*, which gives our full range of products, plus an up-to-date *price list*. If the customer already knows exactly which of our products are required, a *quotation* giving the exact prices is sent. A *tender* or *estimate* are similar but are more often used when installation or work is carried out. The next step is when we wait and hope that an order is placed. Before supplying the goods we sometimes make a *credit enquiry* from a credit reference agency if we're not sure of getting paid. If the customer, for example, needs an import licence, we send a *pro forma invoice*, which is almost identical to the normal invoice.

In situations when the delivery or transit time is really long, an *advice note* is posted. If the goods happen to be transported by road or rail, a *consignment note* is used, if we deliver with our own trucks, a *delivery/despatch note* is issued. Confused?

With the goods, or a short time later, the customer will receive an *invoice* or bill, which is the request for payment. When they're paid, Sharon often mails out a *receipt* *(note that due to his strong German pronunciation Christian does not pronounce this word correctly)*, which is proof of payment.

Sometimes mistakes can happen. In the case where a customer is charged too much, a *credit note* is sent. When the opposite occurs, i.e. the customer is undercharged, a *debit note* is sent.

If the customer is slow in paying, we have to forward a *reminder/collection letter*. Regular customers normally have an account with us and receive a *statement of account* showing what they owe us.

In general our customers are very satisfied. If they're not, they'll make a *complaint* and then it's time for Hazel to explode!"

173 1.

CONTRABAND WHOLESALERS LTD
Wood Quay House
Wood Quay, Manchester GT342
UNITED KINGDOM

Reg. No. 73245
VAT No. RT 3690-867

Tel: 0381 – 6787988
Fax: 0381 – 678989

Ref: JMcE/RK

17 July 20..

Celtic Design Jewellery Limited
Summerhill Industrial Estate
Dublin 24
Ireland

Dear Ms Browne

We *refer* to your advertisement of 6 July in the Irish Manufacturer's Journal and were also most impressed by your *range of products* displayed at the Irish Tourist Information Office in Liverpool.

Contraband is a medium-sized wholesaler *operating* both domestically and internationally and is currently *seeking* a manufacturer who could *supply* us with jewellery for the European teenage market.

As it is our policy *to place* large orders of 5000+ units, we expect an appropriate *quantity discount* in addition to a 15% trade discount off net list-prices. Terms of payment are *negotiable*.

If the above conditions are of interest to you, we would be much *obliged* if you could send us your current catalogue and price-list at your earliest convenience.

Thanking you in *anticipation*.

Yours sincerely
John McEnroy
Chief Buyer

174 2. The students should discuss this in pairs or groups.
Sample solution:
The first paragraph states a reference (in this case to the ad of 6 July and Irish Tourist Information Office).
The second paragraph provides relevant background information of the customer.
The following paragraph states conditions/expectations. As you may notice, in this sample letter the customer is quite demanding.
Paragraph four clarifies future action, i.e. requests CDJ to respond.
The concluding paragraph expresses thanks – something which is sometimes omitted.

3. This is a short enquiry from a private individual, e.g. the student, to a company. It is a free-writing exercise as a prelude to the more guided commercial correspondence exercises that follow.

4. Here students are asked to use the German text as the basis for writing a letter in English.

Wirt & Schmidt GmbH
Am Waldepark 11
13467 Berlin

Ross Systems Ltd
Swallow House
11-21 Greenford Avenue
LONDON
W1N
UK

10 March 20..

Dear Sir or Madam

We refer to a discussion with your representative Ms Lewis at the recent trade fair in Frankfurt. She had promised to send us technical literature about your new MULTIFAX fax machine, which, however, has not reached us so far/up to now.

As we are still very much interested in this fax machine we should/would appreciate if you could send us a quotation (Note: the standard word used)/offer (Note: the more general term) as soon as possible.

If it/the above-mentioned machine meets our requirements, we would be prepared to order substantial quantities. Please inform us about the discounts available/on offer for an order of 100 units and your terms of payment and delivery.

As we need/require the consignment by the end of April at the latest, we would appreciate an early reply.

Yours faithfully

175 TERMS OF PAYMENT AND DELIVERY

This section of the students' book only provides a short explanation of the terms of payment and delivery.

A. TERMS OF PAYMENT

▶ <u>Note:</u> For an explanation of sight draft and after sight draft please refer to p. 189 of the vocabulary list.

A – 1	G – 7	M – 6
B – 4	H – 5	N – 16
C – 2	I – 10	O – 15
D – 9	J – 17	P – 14
E – 3	K – 13	Q – 12
F – 8	L – 11	

177 B. TERMS OF DELIVERY (INCOTERMS)

a) DDP from the D Group
b) EXW from the E Group

178 THE OFFER

1. Make sure that your students are aware that this offer is a response to Contraband's enquiry earlier in this unit.

▶ <u>Note:</u> Commas represent a controversial aspect of English grammar. Their rules and regulations are not always uniform among the various English-speaking countries. There are, however, some fixed rules which should be followed. In these cases, the omissions have been counted as errors.

Celtic Design Jewellery

SUMMERHILL ESTATE, DUBLIN 24, IRELAND

TEL: 01-83564324 (five lines) FAX: 01-85754329 E-MAIL: celtic@design.ie
http://www.celtdes.ie

Contraband Wholesalers Ltd
Wood Quay House
MANCHESTER M13 9PL (This line comes after Wood Quay)
Wood Quay
United Kingdom

24 July 20..

Our Ref: ENQ 544 Your Ref: JMcE/RK

Dear Mr McEnroy

f(F)urther of (to) our telecon (this refers to telephone conversation – it's not a mistake) from (of) today we can confirm, (no comma here – definitely a mistake!) that we are in a position to offer the goods you asked for with a quantity discount of 5% and a revised trade discount of 10%. This means a final prise (price) of € 22,786.90 including VAT, (comma can be used here) which, all in all, (comma before and after this phrase) represents a very well (good) deal for you. As explained, (comma possible here) we would supply an order for 6460 units with the terms of payment being 30 days after receive (receipt) of invoice. We are, of course, (commas possible) prepared to review this and consider open-account terms after a period of regular trading.

Please find enclosed our catalougue (catalogue) and price list. As requested, examples (samples) are included. Prices are ex-works. We look forward to recieve (grammar and spelling incorrect – receiving) your instructions by return.

If you have some (any) further questions, (comma also possible) please do not hesitate to contact us.

Yours faithfully (sincerely)

pp Sharon Steele

Hazel Browne

179 2.

Roscher & Söhne
Radeberger Str. 12
01857 Freital
Germany

Mr Norman
Green & Green
33 Northumberland Rd
BRISTOL BS6 7A2
UK

1 April 20..

Dear Mr Norman

We wish to confirm receipt of your fax/Thank you for your fax of 30 March regarding the supply of/concerning the possibility of supplying special lamps for your production plant in Bath.

We are pleased to note/see that you are interested in our product./Thank you for showing/expressing an interest in our products/product range.

Please find enclosed our catalogue and current price list quoting prices FOB Dresden Airport.

We can/are prepared to grant you a quantity discount of 10% for orders of more than 1,000 units.

Our terms of payment for first/initial orders are cash against documents (CAD)/documents against payment (D/P) payable at Dresdner Bank Freital.

We wish to point out that our delivery period is normally/usually four weeks after receipt of order.

We hope/believe that you will find our conditions/the terms of our offer satisfactory and look forward to hearing from you soon.

Yours sincerely

3. that means/that is	*i.e. (id est)*	179
very important	*NB (nota bene)*	
for example/for instance	*e.g. (exempli gratia)*	
Post Office Box	*POB*	
per procura	*pp*	
et cetera/and so on	*etc*	
pages	*pp*	
namely	*viz. (videlicet)*	
care of	*c/o*	
enclosure(s)	*enc(s)*	
please turn over	*PTO*	
compare	*cf (confer)*	
edited by	*ed.*	
chapter	*ch.*	
see another entry	*q.v. (quod vide) (Note: not S.A.E.)*	
post paid	*pp*	
stamped addressed envelope	*SAE*	
Errors and Omissions Excepted	*E& OE (reserves for the seller the right to correct any error or ommision in the invoice)*	

ECB stands for *European Central Bank, CE (Conformité Européenne)* certifies that products satisfy the requirements of the EU regarding safety, public health, environment and consumer protection.

THE ORDER 180

The correct order is as follows:

1. We confirm receipt ...
2. Please find enclosed ...
3. To ensure that ...
4. Our carrier will arrive ...
5. We look forward to ...

2. 181

Trial order:	The customer <u>orders</u> a small quantity so that he can <u>test</u> the quality.
Firm order:	Here the customer <u>commits</u> himself to <u>buying</u> the goods.
Standing Order:	The customer <u>asks</u> for goods to be <u>delivered</u> in certain quantities at certain intervals.

Merchandise at call:	A large amount of goods is ordered and the customer has specific amounts delivered as he *requires/wants* them.
First/Initial order:	This is the first business *conducted* between the companies.
Advance order:	The goods are ordered a considerable time before customer actually *wants/requires* delivery.
Bulk order:	This is where large amounts are ordered and customers are often *granted* large discounts.
Repeat/Follow-up order:	The customer *reorders* the same goods again.

3. Letter writing

Student's address

Mr Livingstone
Burns Ltd
24-28 Hatch Way
PINNER
Middlesex HA5 4BU
England

Date

Dear Mr Livingstone

Thank you very much for your offer of 5th of this month and the accompanying sample/sample enclosed. (▶ Note: for large samples write: *samples sent separately*) We wish to point out that we were most/very satisfied with the quality of your product.

On condition that you offer us a quantity discount of 15% we would be prepared/willing to place the attached order No. 4731/99.

In this regard we would once again like to express our interest in a long-term business relationship with your company.

We would appreciate a prompt acknowledgement of our order.

Thanking you in anticipation/advance.

Yours sincerely

THE INVOICE

182

Ask your students to study this invoice before attempting to do the exercises on the following page.

▶ Note: The abbreviation *n/a* stands for *not applicable*.

Exercises

1. An invoice (bill BE) is a document issued by a seller to a buyer listing the goods or services supplied and stating the amount due. It is usually prepared on special invoice forms (billheads AE). Cf pro forma invoice and consular invoice. 183

2. Here the students are expected to describe all the invoice details aloud.

3. Conditions of sale, delivery and payment:
   a. Prices are quoted in DM, excluding packaging, Ex Works.
   b. All goods delivered remain the property of the owner until they are fully paid for/off.
   c. Complaints can only be accepted within 8 days on/after receipt of goods.
   d. Prior permission is required from the supplier before goods can be returned and all freight costs must be accepted/borne by the buyer.
   e. Invoices must be paid within 10 days on receipt of invoice at 2% discount or 30 days net.
   f. We reserve the right under certain conditions to demand cash in advance or (payment) guarantees or to rescind the contract.
   g. The above-mentioned conditions are valid for all deliveries.

EXPORT DOCUMENTATION

183 – 184

This exercise provides an overview of important export documents.
The explanation for 2 and 8 as well as 4 and 10 have been swapped. The correct definitions read as follows:

2. Import or Export Licence: Required by governments before goods can be exported or imported.
8. Export Packing List: Prepared by an importer/exporter giving detailed descriptions of goods being sent.
4. Single Administration Document (SAD): Standard document used by EU states in order to eliminate having to use all other forms.
10. Certificate of Insurance: Evidence that the goods are protected against loss or damage.

184 – 186 ADDITIONAL WRITING PRACTICE

This is a series of more challenging exercises for more advanced students. Some of the phrases given in the sample solutions go beyond what is contained in the Reference Section.

184 – Enquiry

1. Make sure that the students understand that Christopher Depp works for Microhard Inc.

Microhard Inc
1472 Bayview Boulevard
Bayview – Florida 33401 – USA

Lynne Computing
73 Irving Place
New York
NY 10003

04/11/01(AE using sample year of 2001)

Ladies and Gentlemen: *or* Dear Sir/Madam:

We refer to your advertisement in last Thursday's issue of OK Computer magazine in which you offered a wide variety of microchips. As an American hardware and software manufacturer we are interested in placing large orders for your products provided terms are satisfactory.

We should be glad if you would send us by return an illustrated catalogue including samples and a price list. Please also state your terms of payment and delivery.

We look forward to receiving an early reply as we should like to make a decision as soon as possible. Thanking you in advance.

Sincerely yours

Christopher Depp
Purchasing Dep.

2. Write the following enquiry. 185

Student's name
c/o S. Machtykova
Roztylske Sady 67
Sporilov
Prague 4
Czech Republic

RTP Classic Bicycle Manufacturers
Craig Industrial Park
Craig Road
CRANBY
Middlesex MX3 5PG
UK

6 July 20..

Dear Sir/Madam

I am intending to open a bicycle store in Prague which will specialise in selling mountain bikes. These are very popular in Prague but there is currently no dealer here that offers a satisfactory range and this is a market gap that I intend to fill. My ten years' experience in bicycle retailing in Swansea, Wales, will also be an advantage.

Therefore, I would be obliged if you could please send me your latest illustrated catalogue and current price list as well as your terms of payment and delivery.

Furthermore, I would like to know whether there are special discounts for start-up businesses and under which conditions you are willing to offer a dealership package. In return, I would be prepared to place regular orders for a guaranteed minimum number of machines, the figure to be mutually agreed.

I look forward to hearing from you at your earliest convenience. Thanking you in anticipation.

Yours faithfully

– Offer

The following points will prove useful for making this offer and should be communicated to students before they commence this letter.

- range of goods available in illustrated catalogue
- price list includes standard terms of payment and delivery
- terms of payment are CWO
- terms of delivery are EXW
- special quantity discount of 6% available
- dealership package only considered after receipt of copy of business plan, references from former employer and name of bank. Appointment in Prague possible after above conditions have been fulfilled.
- long-term business relationship sought

RTP Classic Bicycle Manufacturers
Craig Industrial Park, Craig Road, Cranby, Middlesex MX3 5PG, UK

Student's name
c/o S. Machtykova
Roztylske Sady 67
Sporilov
Prague 4
Czech Republic

22 July 20..

Dear Mr .../Ms ...

Thank you for your enquiry of 6 July which we have carefully considered. Naturally we were very pleased to learn of your interest in our products and, as requested, enclose our illustrated catalogue and price list which includes our range of goods plus standard terms of payment and delivery.

Please note that RTP offers a special quantity discount of 6% for orders exceeding 2,000 units per annum. It is customary that first orders with new clients are on a CWO (cash with order) basis and all prices are EXW (Ex Works) Cranby.

Regarding the question of a dealership package our company usually requests a copy of a business plan, references from your former employer(s) plus the name of a bank which we may refer to. As soon as these matters have been satisfactorily dealt with we would arrange that one of our representatives makes an appointment with you at your premises or prospective premises.

If you have any further questions, please do not hesitate to contact us. We sincerely hope that we are now at the beginning of a long and pleasant business association. We shall certainly do all in our power to make it so.

We look forward to hearing from you.

Yours sincerely

FURNITURE 2000 LTD
Donaldson Road
Dublin 5
Republic of Ireland

Ms Grayson
Barnby & Sons Wholesalers
Strand Road
Derry
Co. Derry
Northern Ireland

5 September 20..

Dear Ms Grayson

We wish to confirm receipt of your letter dated 22 August and are sending you our latest price list. (The prices of the units requested have been highlighted for your added convenience.)

As you have placed regular orders with us in the past, we have decided to allow you a 15% trade discount for all future orders over Stg £10K. Moreover, we are prepared to increase the rate of discount on scales according to each additional Stg £5K of goods purchased.

We hope you will take advantage of this exceptional offer of goods of the very highest quality on/at unusually generous terms and would welcome the opportunity to serve you.

Yours sincerely

– Order

1. Students should note that both companies are situated in the same locality.

Milestone Stores
3 Main Street
Dukesville
CA 15422

Mr J. Lyons
Redneck Inc
Fir Hills
Dukesville
CA 15422

01.02. ..
(or 2 January 20.. or 02/01/..)

Dear Mr Lyons

Due to the unusually cold winter period and resulting high demand we are placing an additional order (see attached) for 270 superior-quality thermal winter jackets.

This is a matter of great urgency as our stocks are fast running out, so we would ask you to deliver within the next 48 hours and charge to our account.

We apologize for any inconvenience caused and are prepared to forgo (to do without) any additional discounts you may have offered for such a large order.

Please kindly acknowledge this order and confirm that you will be able to make this deadline.

Thanking you in advance.

Sincerely yours

186 2.

Hardcastle Engineering
Durrant Road, East Kilbride, Edinburgh, UK

Zorbac Manufacturing
ul. Batorego 67
02-591 Warsaw
Poland

25 May 20..

Dear Mr Mickiewicz

Much to our regret a strike of dock workers in Glasgow is resulting in delays in the despatch of a number of consignments to our customers. We are sorry to have to inform you that the set of machine tools ordered by yourselves on 13 March is among those being held up.

We made arrangements to have the consignment diverted to Liverpool but, unfortunately, the dock workers there are refusing to handle any of the goods involved in the dispute as a mark of solidarity with their Glasgow counterparts.

Both the employers and the trade unions representing the dockers are currently in negotiations and we are hoping for a successful outcome from these talks.

We deeply apologise for the delay and hope that you will understand that it is entirely due to causes outside our control.

Yours sincerely

Simulation

This simulation is primarily computer-oriented and can be done either in a computer lab or from home. If the latter is chosen the instructor should check printouts for language accuracy and appropriateness. Should your group lack access to computers the simulation activity can be done in a classroom situation as a letter writing activity.
The simulation can be continued with the complaint after the first part of Unit 11 has been completed.

Story Line

After more than three months in business Celtic Design Jewellery is doing fine. There are, however, some problems concerning the staff that have to be solved. Sharon is not very punctual and customers have been complaining about other members of staff. Hazel calls a meeting and invites a friend of hers, Paul Taylor, to give a talk on Cultural Awareness as her business is going more international.

Ray Connors, the insurance friend, is a big part of Hazel's private life at the moment. She wonders how serious Ray is about her.

Focus

- To raise the awareness of cultural differences
- To introduce and practise the language of meetings
- To enable students to make and adjust a complaint in English
- To compare British and American English vocabulary and spelling

A COMPLAINT *193 – 194*

After explaining that there is a problem at CDJ ask your group to read through the fax and find out what has happened. Before turning to the exercises students should familiarise themselves with the language of complaints (p. 279).

Discussion/Exercises *194*

1. Students are invited to refer to their own or friends' experience.

2. Problems could be wrong quantity, wrong colour, poor quality, late delivery, damage, faulty goods or bad packaging.

3. In general, organisations replace goods, offer refunds, give credit notes, etc.

4.

Dear Mr .../Ms ...

Re: Order No. 103/69

We regret to have to inform you that yesterday's consignment/the consignment we received yesterday does not correspond with the above order.

Ten of the lamps are not the desired size and, furthermore, two are of a different colour. We have, therefore, decided to return the unrequested units and expect immediate replacements.

Moreover/In addition, we would like to point out that problems in quality regarding your consignment of July 12 have resulted in us having difficulties with certain customers.

In the future, we expect that you will comply with the contract conditions, otherwise we will be forced to find a new supplier.

Yours sincerely

195

5.

Mahon Ltd   54 Hickson Road   Millers Point   NSW 2000   Australia

Our Ref:
Order 18/503   Your Ref: Ms T.   20..-09-01

Dear Ms Telford

We acknowledge delivery of your printing machine which we received yesterday.

However, we regret to have to inform you that the printing quality is not up to the required standard.

Moreover, the packaging was open on arrival at our premises but this may have occurred in transit.

We are prepared to keep the machine provided an engineer is sent immediately to rectify the situation. Otherwise, we will be forced to return the consignment.

We look forward to hearing from you as soon as possible.

Yours sincerely

6. This letter refers to the complaint addressed to Mr Donovan (p. 194). 194

Celtic Design Jewellery

SUMMERHILL ESTATE, DUBLIN 24, IRELAND

TEL: 01-83564324 (five lines) FAX: 01-85754329 E-MAIL: celtic@design.ie
http://www.celtdes.ie

Sloweys
Head Office
Nelson House
Portland Street
LONDON EC17BQ

1 September 20..

Our Ref: JD/SS Your Ref: DW/NJ
Order No. S11733 CDJ

Dear Ms Walters

We were extremely sorry to receive your complaint concerning the above order and deeply regret any inconvenience caused.

The reason for this unfortunate situation was caused by a mix-up error as explained by my telephone call of yesterday.

In order to rectify this/the problem we have already arranged the immediate despatch of the missing 450 items this morning.

We trust that the arrangements we have made will satisfy you and assure you that this will not happen again.

Yours sincerely

John Donovan

John Donovan

Deliveries Section

Answerphone Messages

Samples:

Hello, you have reached Nora Gilroy on 8222431. Please leave your name and number plus a short message after the beep. I'll ring back as fast as I can. Thanks and goodbye!

This is Brennan's Plastic Ltd. Our office is presently closed so nobody is available to answer your call. Please leave your name, number and any message after the bleep. Your call will be returned as soon as possible. Thank you.

▶ Note: *Beep* or *bleep* are both used.

196 – 205 THE MEETING

Before listening to the meeting, explain to your learners the different kinds of meetings held in companies. Informal meetings are called at short notice to discuss matters which arise suddenly. Unlike formal meetings they have no accompanying agenda, and often no minutes or written record is kept.

Students should refer to Meetings (pp. 296–298) in the Reference Section.

196 A. DISCUSSING COMPLAINTS

1. The various parts of the agenda should be looked through and discussed.

2. This is another listening exercise requiring the students to keep their books closed. The six questions should be put on the board or dictated before commencing the exercise.
   a) The main items are the complaints problem and a talk about Cultural Awareness.
   b) Sloweys, one of their main customers, has made a complaint concerning an incomplete delivery of the DA8 line. (Instead of 4610 units 4160 were sent.) John, who is responsible, is told to send them a fax and apologise again. In future deliveries should be checked twice to avoid similar problems.
   c) Christian was chatting with Sharon while Hazel was speaking.
   d) Martin, a young colleague, received a phone call from Karstadt in Germany and was unable to answer their questions. Obviously he had problems with the language and, moreover, didn't know all the details the customer was interested in. He should have offered to get Christian, a German, or another competent person to call them back. The customer is the king!

e) By VIP treatment Hazel means that everything has to be done to please the customer, by taking him out for a nice meal and whatever else he might be interested in doing.
f) The advantage is that they are able to deal with these customers directly, without agents or wholesalers.

▶ Note: *MBWA = Management by walking about,* i.e. the management go around the shop floor to observe what's happening and are not restricted to paperwork in the offices.

B. A TALK ON CULTURAL AWARENESS

As an introduction it's a good idea to ask students to discuss aspects of their own culture and how they imagine they are perceived by people from other countries. The discussion could refer to the image, punctuality, general behaviour, reputation of products, corporate culture, communication styles etc.

Alternatively this can be dealt with after listening to Paul Taylor's talk (p. 203 no. 7 or p. 208 no. 6).

The first part of Paul Taylor's talk gives students a basic understanding of the hidden dimensions of cultural differences.

The cassette may need to be played twice as it is relatively demanding and students have to listen for specific details. In weaker groups this can also be done as a reading exercise.

Part One – True or False? *199*

1. F (Paul is still at the company – difference between Past Simple and Present Perfect.)
2. F (He had taken part in a project investigating cultural diversity.)
3. F (Culture is described as an iceberg.)
4. F (It is the first dimension he discusses.)
5. T
6. F (The opposite is true.)
7. F (These are weak countries in this category.)
8. T
9. T
10. T

201 **Part Two**

This section shows the more visible aspects of culture including personal experiences with people from other countries. It's done as a listening exercise requiring closed books. The two questions should be put on the board/OHP or dictated before commencing the exercise.

1. Critical areas:
- the concept of time (punctuality is important in northern European countries and the USA but less important in southern Europe, Ireland and Scotland),
- the agenda of meetings may be tight (USA) or open (Latin America, Middle East),
- the time needed before getting down to business (in Saudi Arabia and other Gulf states building up a relationship before negotiations is seen as vital but may be extremely time-consuming),
- directness (valued in the USA, harmony and group consensus are important in Japan)
- managers who are either generalists (Britain, Ireland) or specialists (Germany)
- socialising (including alcohol consumption, dress styles, making gifts)
- body language (gestures may have different meanings, patterns of eye contact and conversational distance vary from country to country)

2. Watch what is happening around you, inform yourself, be careful, use your common sense, avoid stereotyping and don't misinterpret personality differences as cultural ones.

203 **Discussion**

The topic of cultural differences lends itself to a multitude of different opinions and often controversial discussions.

C. AOB

This is an opportunity for students to practise taking minutes with books remaining closed. Afterwards, ask them to compare results with one another or check the transcript.

Sample Minutes:

AOB
- Staff punctuality. Employees are expected to be punctual. Work starts at 8.30 every day. (Hazel)
- Report on the interim balance sheet (Sharon)
- Holidays: At the moment only one person can take holidays at any one time (John)
- Christmas Party: Takes place at Jury's Hotel (majority of votes)
- New design for SF 352: Discussion postponed.

THE LANGUAGE OF MEETINGS

205 – 206

Students go through Parts A (pp. 197–199) and C (pp. 203–205) of the meeting and fill in relevant phrases under the appropriate headings.

A Starting/Opening the meeting
Right, as we are all here let's make a start.

B Establishing the targets
The two main points for today's meeting are ...

C Asking for contributions/Involving the participants
Any comments or questions ...? / Over to you. / Would you like to add anything? /
(Sharon), I think you wanted to say something? / What's on your mind? /
Allow me to introduce ... / Anyway, over to you ... / Would you talk us through this ... /
Could you open this one? / ... any takers ... / We haven't heard from you yet ... .
What do you think?

D Paraphrasing/Clarifying
So, have you all got a copy of the agenda? / As you can see ... /
So, what you're saying is ... / What exactly do you mean by that? /
OK that means I, as chairperson, have the casting vote. /
I'm sorry. I didn't hear what you said. Would you mind repeating it ...?

E Interrupting
Excuse me ... but

F Dealing with Interruptions
Would you mind addressing your remarks to the chair rather than to ... ?

G Slowing down a meeting
n/a

H Moving a meeting on
So, next, the minutes of the last meeting. / OK, on to item 4 ...
Let's move on to the next point. / I'll be brief and to the point.
But we're running short of time. So, could you please be fairly quick?
... the next item on the agenda concerns ... / Very well then, last point ...

205 – 206 **I Dealing with digressions**

I think we'd better leave that subject for another time.

J Proposing

I absolutely agree with you (supporting a proposal) / I suggest that we take the points ... / I propose ... .

So, can we have a vote?

So, Sharon's proposal has been accepted by ... . to ... . (Wynn's) has been rejected.

K Summarising

So, to summarise what has been said so far ...

L Closing/Ending the meeting

That just about covers everything. / The next meeting will be... /

206 CULTURAL STEREOTYPING & VARIATIONS

1. This is a preparation for the reading text that follows.

2. Ask the students to read the text 'How to behave in Germany' and choose the correct headline from the list A – H for each part of the text (1) – (8).

1 = B	5 = F
2 = G	6 = H
3 = A	7 = E
4 = C	8 = D

208 Exercises 3., 4., and 6. continue the theme of stereotyping and reflection on culture.

5. The words in italics are all American English:
   schedule = plan (BE)
   organization with 'z' compared to BE *organisation*
   vacations = holidays (BE)
   humor without 'u' as in BE *humour*
   check = bill (BE)
   gray spelt with 'a' compared to BE *grey*

7. 209

AE		BE	AE		BE
downtown	=	centre	check (restaurant)	=	bill
subway	=	underground	elevator	=	lift
gasoline	=	petrol	truck	=	lorry
fall	=	autumn	eraser	=	rubber
freeway	=	motorway	cookie	=	biscuit
streetcar	=	tram	schedule	=	timetable
bill	=	bank note	lawyer	=	solicitor
trashcan	=	dustbin	instalment plan	=	hire purchase
mail	=	post	public holiday	=	bank holiday
janitor	=	caretaker	labor union	=	trade union

Vocabulary check 210

1. Another word for a delivery of goods. *consignment*
2. The programme for a meeting. *agenda*
3. To generalise about a country or its people. *stereotype*
4. No movement in a traffic jam or negotiation. *gridlock*
5. A short talk is a *brief* talk.
6. American English for present (noun). *gift*
7. To repay expenses. *reimburse*
8. The negotiations may end in *stalemate* when neither side is willing to compromise.
9. The wholesaler often sells on to the *retailer* who sells on to the customer.
10. A formal proposal to be discussed and voted on. *motion*
11. The abbreviations AOB and MBWA stand for *Any Other Business* and *Management By Walking About.*
12. A synonym for adjusting a complaint. *settling*
13. Showing bias. *prejudice*
14. To offend. *insult*
15. To make a formal statement of support for a proposal made by someone else at a meeting. to second

Simulation

A Staff Meeting: A question of discrimination?

The activity can be spiced up even more by getting one or two of the students to act as journalists at a press conference with the company Public Relations Officer and the person claiming discrimination.

Story Line

Hazel is on a business trip to the Leipzig Fair in Germany. Ray had promised to come but pulled out. Her German friends Silke and Rudi were not waiting for her at Leipzig Central Station when she arrived. When they finally did arrive they returned to their flat. The trade fair itself is successful. The return journey proves to be an eventful one.

Focus

- To discuss the economic situation of Germany and expand this into students' own country/region/city/locality.
- To gain an insight into and practise the steps in a sales talk
- To role-play travel situations including giving directions

216 THE LEIPZIG E-MAIL

even though – because – Unfortunately – anyway – as well – so – only – because – Actually — either – Of course – so.

GERMANY AND SAXONY – AN OVERVIEW

This unit is relatively short but should be supplemented by current material on Germany.

218 Comprehension

A. Germany is a member of the G8, i.e. one of the 8 major industrial countries, holding third place in overall economic performance and second place with regard to world trade. Its GDP has doubled in the past 30 years.

B. The success was possible because of Germany's skilled manpower, their training, industry, and managerial skills, and the effects of the social market economy.

C. For him it was not a miracle, Germany's rapid development was purely the result of honest endeavour on the part of the whole nation.

D.
- Leipzig: 508,000 inhabitants, 'Little Paris', Centre of peaceful resistance to the East German regime, location for international trade fairs.
- Dresden: 488,000 inhabitants, 'Florence on the Elbe', capital of the Free State of Saxony, was almost totally destroyed in 1945, cultural centre with famous Opera House and fine museums, University of Technology, centre of high-tech industries.
- Chemnitz: Has a technical university, centre of mechanical engineering and micro-electronics.

- Zwickau: Car manufacturing centre, formerly for the Trabant, now for Volkswagen production.

Discussion 218

A. "GNP" stands for "Gross National Product", the value of all goods and services produced by the residents of a state, including profits earned abroad. "GDP" is the abbreviation for "Gross Domestic Product", the value of all goods and services produced within a state but excluding profits earned abroad.

B. The abbreviation "G8" stands for "Group of 8" and refers to the eight most advanced industrialised nations in the world. It is sometimes referred to as G7 + Russia. The original G7 members were U.K., U.S.A., Canada, France, Germany, Italy, and Japan.

C. In a "market economy" the economic decisions are taken by private individuals who own the factors of production. This type of economy is often referred to as a free enterprise economy, capitalist or free enterprise system. The USA is a classic example.

The term "centrally planned economy" describes an economic system in which all decisions are taken by the government. In addition to this, the government claims ownership of the factors of production. This is often referred to as a controlled or socialist economy. Examples are the former USSR and North Korea.

A "social market economy" or "mixed economy" aims to have the best of both of the other two kinds of economic models, i.e. some elements of state ownership coupled with free enterprise. This model also offers a safety net for the underprivileged sections of society. Countries of the European Union provide examples of this although the tendency is to develop towards a free enterprise economy. This development can be seen through the process of privatisation of state assets such as railway, telecommunication, water and power supply systems.

D. This can be done as a short presentation activity to be prepared at home.

YOUTH REALITIES 219

1 – b
2 – c (Lithuania is the only non-EU country in this list)
3 – c
4 – c
5 – c
6 – a

220 **Discussion**

This exercise should be prepared as homework as the students will need to inform themselves about current economic data.

221 AT THE TRADE FAIR

1. This can be done as a lead-in. Students could be asked about the products presented, whether/why they liked the fair/didn't like it, if there are students who have already worked at a fair and what job they had to do, etc.

2. In this exercise students are put in at the deep-end and role-play the situation without any previous preparation. After having done the model sales talk (3) and following the discussion of the steps (4) they should repeat this role-play activity (5).

3. Students should be asked to list the different steps in Hazel's sales pitch. The first two in the sample solution can be given as a guideline. It's recommended to play the piece twice.

   Sample Solution:
   - Greeting
   - Offering help
   - Offering something to drink
   - Finding out potential customer's name
   - Introducing oneself
   - Enquiring about customer wants
   - Finding out customer's line of business
   - Offering and promoting own range of products
   - Initiating further contacts (catalogue & card)
   - Closing conversation politely

222
4. First students compare and discuss the different steps in their own and Hazel's sales talk. Then they should underline key phrases from the above tapescript that correspond to a-g.

5. Now repeat the role-play as in exercise 2. With the knowledge students have acquired via the steps in a sales talk the approach will probably be more focused.

6. Many answers are possible including personal appearance and approach, location of stand, attractiveness of display, technical equipment, sample materials, etc.

Vocabulary check

1. A long-term break for a mother when her child is born. *maternity leave*
2. Germany's economy was built on skilled *labour.*
3. Scotland is sparsely populated but Hong Kong is *densely* populated.
4. German products have a good *reputation.*
5. Another word for goods. *merchandise*
6. Free trade doctrine. *Laissez-faire*
7. There is a trend away from *manufacturing* towards service industries.
8. Increasing numbers or *swelling* ranks of unemployed.
9. Another term for world economy. *Global economy*
10. VAT stands for *Value Added Tax.*
11. Another word for precondition also starting with pre-. *prerequisite*
12. To improve equipment. *upgrade*
13. Extremely important. *crucial*
14. A *summit* was held between EU heads of state in Brussels.
15. Organisation representing employees' interests. *trade union*

Simulation 223

The groups in this simulation could organise a trade fair where diverse businesses meet. Promotional material from the simulation in Unit 5 (Advertising) can be used.

TRAVEL SITUATIONS

Role-plays

These are guided role-plays for face-to-face Social English and telephone situations. Please refer to the Reference Section if necessary.

Asking for Directions 224

▶ Note: Students should consult the Reference Section (p. 294) for this part.

1. Queen Mary's Hospital is left of centre in the map, Putney Bridge Underground Station is on the top right hand corner of the map, Wimbledon Common is on the lower middle part and Richmond is on the top left corner.

Students can exchange roles in order to practise asking for and giving directions.

2. This represents another role-play where students work in pairs.

Story Line

Hazel has to deal with the book-keeping although she detests it. The balance sheet has to be prepared with the help of Sharon, the secretary. Hazel gets a reminder from the tax office that her tax return is overdue.

Focus

- To introduce accountancy terminology and a balance sheet
- To look at the essentials of taxation
- To practise numbers and figures

227 – 228 **THE BALANCE SHEET**

A. ACCOUNTING TERMS

Give students time to read the explanations of accounting terms before they do the gap-filling exercise.

1. fixed assets
2. balance
3. turnover
4. debtor, creditor
5. net profit
6. gross profit
7. current assets
8. current liabilities

229 **B. THE INTERIM BALANCE SHEET**

1. See overleaf for the completed balance sheet.

2. *Fixed assets* are long term, *current assets* are always changing and can be quickly converted into cash. Another term used for *long-term liabilities* is *fixed liabilities*.

Balance Sheet 31.10.20..

Current Assets		
Stock	18,898 *	
Debtors	***12,421***	
Bank Balance	3,250	
Cash in Hand	600	
TOTAL CURRENT ASSETS		35,169
* at cost price		
Fixed Assets		
Machinery	40,000	
Vehicles	***10,154***	
Fixtures and Fittings	12,750	
TOTAL FIXED ASSETS		62,904
TOTAL ASSETS		**98,073**
Current Liabilities		
Creditors	12,400	
Tax to be paid	***1,985***	
Bank Overdraft	4,015	
TOTAL CURRENT LIABILITIES		18,400
Long -Term Liabilities		
Bank Loan	45,000	
TOTAL LONG-TERM LIABILITIES		45,000
TOTAL LIABILITIES		63,400
Capital and Reserves		
H.Browne (At start)	***36,457***	
Profit & Loss A/C	- 1,784	
NET WORTH OF BUSINESS		34,673
TOTAL LIABILITIES & CAPITAL RESERVES		**98,073**

TAXATION

A. A LETTER FROM THE TAX OFFICE

1.

A. The tax return has to be submitted without delay.

B. In this case the surcharge will be increased to 10% on her tax liability. She can also face prosecution.

C. This should happen if she was not obliged to file a tax return or has already submitted one and also if she needs help.
See overleaf for the completed balance sheet.

2. 230

submit = send in/enter	return = statement	remittance = payment
outstanding = overdue	incurred = earned	obliged = required
prior = previous	prosecuted = taken to court	on your behalf = for you
file = enter/send in	due = payable	

B. THE TAX GUIDE

232 – 233

Referring to the opening paragraph allow students a few minutes to discuss their attitude towards tax evasion.

1. Ask students to read the excerpt from the tax guide (p. 233).
   are employed; increases; rises
   are (further) classified
   reduce; are required; is deducted; are also subtracted; sends
   are obliged; is given
   levied; are allowed; be paid
   is charged; sold
   is applied; take place
   are paid; include; is obliged
   involve

▶ Note: *PAYE* stands for *Pay As you Earn* while in the USA there is a *PAYG* system, i.e. *Pay As You Go*. These are forms of direct taxation where the employer deducts the appropriate amount of tax from employees' gross wages or salaries at source, i.e. the employee receives his/her earnings less tax.

2. This is a consolidation exercise using the vocabulary, p. 233.

   a) salary
   b) social insurance
   c) indirect
   d) VAT
   e) progressive
   f) regressive
   g) corporation tax
   h) inheritance
   i) exempt
   j) tax
   k) fined, prison
   l) tax return

3. This question may only be appropriate where the students have some knowledge of their taxation system. It should be approached only after 1 and 2 have been attempted.

NUMBERS & FIGURES

234

A. Refer to Measurements and Numbers (pp. 302–304) in the Reference Section beforehand if necessary.

4. Stg£ is officially referred to as Pounds Sterling.
11. M-dot-Schils-at-arnhem-dot-peters-dot-nl
    h-t-t-p-colon-double slash-w-w-w-dot-d-k-m-dot-i-e-slash-events.
16. Fifteen love
18. The picture is two feet seven inches by five feet eight and a half inches.

235

B. European Union: euro
USA: dollar
Japan: yen
Russia: rouble

C. a. 80÷4=20 or 80÷20=4
b. 1l = 1.76pts
c. 2/3
d. 2-1
e. 1978
f. 1603
g. 99 60 73
h. 70 45 28
i. 47.5%
j. Ref. no. 66/29-4
k. 5x5=25
l. 40-15+8=33
m. 30°C i.e. 86°F
n. 30:0
o. 2-2
p. 7.35pm on 9th September
q. $6.50
r. € 6,489,570
s. 4' 2 3/4'' x 2' 8 1/2''
t. 1/4

Optional exercise

236

Calculating Income Tax

This is quite a complicated exercise and should only be attempted by stronger students. They should read Numbers (pp. 303–304) in advance. Instructors should explain the income tax guidelines (p. 236) and the following notes.

▶ Note:
- This particular exercise focuses on the annual obligatory income tax return for employees (not self-employed).
- The €4,200 allowance is the total for a married couple and is granted regardless of whether one or two partners are working.
- The full State Social Insurance allowance of € 572 and the full PAYE allowance of €1,600 is only valid when both partners are working. SSI in Ireland only covers dental and optical care in state-run institutions which are often under-funded. You must pay to visit a doctor or go to hospital, which is why many people take out an extra voluntary health insurance (VHI) policy which is fully tax-deductible.
- Life Assurance is not tax-deductible.
- Pension payments are 100% tax-deductible of gross salary (not income) only.
- Mortgage interest relief is also deductible against gross salary (not income) only.
- *p.a.* stands for *per annum.*
- *PAYE* stands for *Pay As you Earn* while in the USA there is a *PAYG* system, i.e. *Pay As You Go*. These are forms of direct taxation where the employer deducts the appropriate amount of tax from employees' wages or salaries at source, i.e. the employee receives his/her earnings less tax.

Students should do the calculations on paper and then read out the results to the class as it's a good exercise in reading figures aloud. Students can also calculate weekly tax liability in each case.

237 **Computation 1**

The two errors are:
1. SSI allowance or relief is €286 and not €268.
2. Taxable income of €8,794 is calculated @ 27% and not @ 48% as they are married, i.e. first €14,950 @ 27%.

Robert has an annual salary and income of €17,000.
Allowances:
€4,200 = married allowance
€800 = PAYE allowance
€286 = SSI allowance
€1,000 = VHI allowance
=€1,920 = 80% of €2,400 mortgage interest on home
€8,206
€17,000 - €8,206 = €8,794 = taxable income of €8,794 @ 27% = €2,374.38 p.a. (÷ 52 = €45.66 per week).

Computation 2

Julia has an annual income of € 34,000, i.e. a salary of € 30,000 plus € 4,000 in benefit-in-kind for her car.

Allowances:

€4,200 = married allowance
€800 = PAYE allowance
€286 = SSI allowance (her husband is unemployed)
€3,200 = 80% of €4,000 mortgage interest on home
€800 = VHI allowance
=€1,500 = 5% of salary as pension contribution
€10,786
€34,000 - €10,786 = taxable income of €23,214

First €14,950 is calculated @ 27% = €4,036.50
Balance of €8,264 @ 48% = €3,966.72.

Tax liability is €8,003.22 (÷ 52 = €153.90 per week).

Computation 3

Explain that students should do a single tax return for the couple (not two separate returns).

Mr and Mrs Johnson have a combined annual income of €37,000, i.e. salaries of €14,000 + €18,000 plus €5,000 benefit in kind.

Allowances:

€4,200 = married allowance
€1,600 = PAYE allowance (both working)
€572 = SSI allowance (both working)
€2,880 = 80% mortgage interest relief of €3,600
€1,200 = VHI allowance
€1,600 = 5% as pension contribution
=€12,052
€37,000 - €12,052 = taxable income of €24,948.

First €14,950 is calculated @ 27% = €4,036.50
Balance of €9,998 @ 48% = €4,799.04

Tax liability is €8,835.54 p.a.
(÷ 52 = €169.91 per week).

238 MORE TELEPHONING

1. It's a really bad line so, can you speak up please?
   I've been trying to contact you for hours.
   Please leave a message on the answerphone.
   I'm ringing concerning the Ryan contract.
   I'm afraid he is not available at the moment.
   Would you like me to ask her to phone you back?

238 – 239 2. The role-plays focus on complaining and problem-solving.

239 **Simulation**

Here students can search the Internet to find company balance sheets in order to help them devise their own. Allow them to be very creative in reducing their tax bill.

Story Line

Hazel has already signed a leasing contract for her computers with Livingstone Computers but has unfortunately forgotten to include the maintenance side. She now requires a service contract and has to negotiate with Patrick Gormley of Livingstone Computers. Patrick comes to negotiate with her in a strong position as he knows she will be more or less forced to accept his conditions – she hasn't really got a choice.

Focus

- To practise negotiation skills
- To read and understand a contract
- To understand basic computer terminology

A NEGOTIATION

243 – 244

At first students should read the introduction which is setting the scene for the main part.

1. This is the negotiation scene. Ask your students to take notes while listening.
   Patrick Gormley from Livingstone computers has arrived to negotiate a service contract with Hazel, who is unprepared and leaves him waiting for a few minutes. She had received the draft beforehand which, however, didn't state the price.

   Patrick informs her that the price is € 3000 a month which according to him is fair for the amount of equipment that Hazel has leased. Hazel is shocked. In her opinion the computer system is too complex for the needs of her business, but she has to learn that it is neither possible to change anything at this stage nor is Pat willing to make any allowance.

   Hazel's idea to contact another company is turned down by Patrick who points out that it is unusual to lease the equipment from one company and have it serviced by another. This would make it even more expensive.

   Before making a decision Hazel wants to discuss the deal with a member of her staff who is not available the whole day.

   For Patrick the price represents the bottom line and he insists on Hazel signing the draft on the same day. Otherwise it would be impossible for him to hold the price.
   He makes vague promises for the next leasing agreement. Hazel is disappointed and indicates that this may have been the last time dealing with Livingstone for her.

UNIT 14 NEGOTIATING A CONTRACT

245 Discussion

Students refer to Negotiating (pp. 298-300).

a) This was a win-lose with Hazel in a losing situation.

b) Here are some ideas referring to the dos and don'ts:

- Hazel didn't have a clear idea of what she wanted.
- She hadn't planned ahead for this meeting.
- She didn't make any offers.
- She didn't manage to end positively.
- She also made things easy for the other party.
- She got stuck in a corner.
- Hazel went ahead and did a big deal alone.

c) Students can do this exercise alone or in pairs using the negotiating steps (pp. 299-300).

(Relationship building)

H: Pat! Sorry for keeping you waiting.
PG: No problem. So, how's life?
H: I'm up to my eyes. It's just non-stop around here. And yourself?
PG: I'm kept going.
H: Good. Good.

(Agreeing the procedure)

PG: So, Hazel, let's make a start. ... I thought it better to put down something on paper rather than starting from scratch.

(Stating position)

What I'm looking for is to come to a fair arrangement.

(Attempting to clarify ...)

H: ... So, how much are we talking about here?

(Coercion/Emotion)

PG: I understand, Hazel, but unfortunately there's nothing I can do.
H: Honestly, I'd really like to give you the business, but for that price, I may have to look elsewhere.
PG: Ehh ... to tell you the truth, Hazel ... You'll be hit with a bigger bill – believe me. Of course, you're welcome to try.
H: Hmm ...

(Looking at options)

PG: ... What I'm trying to say is that you're miles better off staying with us given your current situation, both from a service and financial point of view.

(Coercion/Emotion)

PG: Look, Hazel, I'm really trying to help you here. ... I can't improve that price. It's the bottom line.

(Playing for time)

H: Well, I'll have to discuss it with Mr Birke ...

(Avoid playing for time/Coercion)

PG: I understand, but I'm afraid that I can't hold that price. I'll need your signature on that draft today. **(Proposal)** How about this? You accept my offer and we can work something out when you negotiate your next leasing agreement.

H: ... (Coercion) I'm not even sure I will be dealing with your company next time round.

PG: (Playing for time) Hazel, I can't give you any figures at the moment because it's too far ahead ...

Role-plays

For the role-plays the students can refer, if necessary, to Social English as well as to Negotiating in the Reference Section.

THE CONTRACT

246

Comprehension

1. Ask your students to read the contract (pp. 247–248) carefully before attempting this exercise.

Para I
A. F (See 1.)
B. T (See 3.)

Para II
A. T (See 2.)
B. T (See 3.)
C. T (See 5.)
D. F (See 6. *endeavour* is not a guarantee)
E. F (See 7.)

Para III
A. F (See 1. *retains the right to adjust*)
B. F (See 3.)
C. F (See 2.)

Para IV
A. T (See 1.)
B. T (See 2.)

Para V
A. T (See 1.)

Para VI
A. T (The indications are that this is a standard contract as per the preamble. If the contract is longer, it would be specified in the Appendix. In this case, there is no Appendix).
B. T (See 2. – the contract was signed on 20 October)

2. Here students are asked to analyse the text.
   Answers include the following:
   - use of passive voice
   - frequent use of gerund, infinitives, participles
   - use of 'shall' to indicate conditions of a contract
   - formal language
   - words of Latin origin
   - no phrasal verbs or colloquialisms

249 COMPUTER TERMINOLOGY

Many students have problems identifying key computer terminology. Here's a selection (but remember things can change very fast in this field).

1. Many people like to spend their evenings s**urfing**/s**earching** the Internet; you can do it with the help of a programme called W**eb**-b**rowser** (or Webclient). Interesting information from the Internet can be do**wnloaded** onto your computer.
2. If your software is not correctly installed, your computer could c**rash**. Problems in programmes can be also caused by bu**gs**, software can be infected by v**iruses**.
3. The screen is part of the m**onitor**. In addition, there are computer peripherals such as the k**eyboard**, p**rinter**, m**ouse** and the s**peaker**/s**canner**. These are all referred to as h**ardware**. The computer is connected via a m**odem** to the telephone line.
4. In most computers a d**isk (BE)**/d**isc (AE)** is a primary means of storing data. Types of disks used with computers include fl**oppy** disks, c**ompact** discs (optical discs) and **hard** disks. A device that reads from and writes to disks is called a disk d**rive**. A disk can contain a large number of f**iles**, which can be organised in dir**ectories** (folders).
5. A computer is said to be co**mpatible** if it can use hardware and software specifications that have become standard in the computing industry.

6. A set of application programs for work might contain a word pr**ocessing** programme, a sp**readsheet**, a datab**ase** ma**nagement** programme, and a com**munications** programme.
7. In a word-processing programme using a mouse, it is possible to dr**ag** a section of text to another position and dr**op** it there.
8. To see more of the contents of a text, sc**roll** the screen to the next section. If you have several documents open at the same time, you can display them one on top of the other so that the title bar of each wi**ndow** is visible, i.e. ca**scade** them.
9. A graphical us**er** int**erface** (GUI) represents programmes, files, and options by means of ic**ons** and me**nus** on the screen. The user can select and activate these options by poi**nting** and cli**cking** with a mouse or with the keyboard.
10. You can copy a part of a text into the temporary memory or cli**pboard**, later you can pas**te** it into the desired position.

Vocabulary check 250

1. The first written version of a contract. *draft*
2. Period of two weeks. *fortnight*
3. To prolong a contract. *extend*
4. For the benefit of both sides, i.e. *mutual* benefit.
5. Payment. *remuneration*
6. To put something into effect. *implement*
7. To discuss or talk to reach an agreement. *negotiate*
8. Legal regulations. *statutory provisions*
9. Term used showing that someone has broken a condition of a contract. *breach of contract*
10. To settle a contract. *conclude*

Simulation

This simulation may break the flow of events which started with the simulation exercise in Unit 3. Instructors should feel free to use other negotiation situations than the one offered in the students' book.

A POEM 251

Students give creative answers!

Story Line

Celtic Design Jewellery is flying with lots of overtime expected from all members of staff. Hazel has great plans for the company. Christian Birke, her marketing assistant, has to check out a potential merger with Farrington Jewellery Products, which after careful scrutiny is rejected.

On New Year's Eve Hazel is still at work. She is in contemplative mood.

Focus

- To discuss the world of mergers and takeovers
- To prepare and write a business report

MERGERS

256 **BUSINESS FOCUS**

The Daimler-Benz and Chrysler merger represents the first truly global merger that took place. Analysts rated it initially as one of the better merger success stories although conflicts have occurred at a managerial and cultural level. Students should find out the latest state of affairs including the share price.

▶ Note: Weaker students may need a dictionary for some parts of this unit.

257 **Comprehension/Discussion**

1. Reasons for Daimler: Strong competition; competitors were encroaching on their traditional territory; lower profit margins; problems with their small cars, which could tarnish the company's image
   Reasons for Chrysler: Over-proportional production of trucks; vans and sports utility vehicles; car sales had fallen considerably and the company had been overtaken by competitors; underdeveloped international market
   Other general reasons include:
   - synergies, i.e. companies produce greater overall effects by joining forces rather than acting separately. (Synergy is usually expressed as the 2+2 = 5 effect meaning that the sum is greater than the total of the parts).
   - cost savings, i.e. economies of scale
   - increased market share
   - increased creditworthiness
   - combined Research and Development (R&D)
   - more marketing expertise

2. A *merger* is the voluntary coming together of two companies, often, but not always, in the same industry. A Japanese example is the merger of Mazda and Mitsubishi, both primarily car manufacturers. In a *joint venture* two or more companies/countries agree to co-operate on a special project whereas in a *takeover* or *acquisition* one company acquires at least 51% of another company, thereby taking control. This can often be aggressive compared to the voluntary, co-operative pattern of a merger. Some can actually be *friendly*, i.e. Rover was glad to be taken over by BMW. Often they are *hostile*, i.e. Vodafone and Mannesmann at the beginning.

3. Students check latest business news.
   Examples include Germany: Hertie and Karstadt (takeover), USA: AOL and Time Warner (merger), Glaxo Wellcome and SmithKLine Beecham (merger of drug companies).

4. Sample answers include:
   - Fewer and bigger multinationals dominate the world economy
   - Increasing trend towards conglomerates (large corporation consisting of a group of companies dealing in a wide range of goods and/or services, e.g. General Electric)
   - Trend towards oligopolies (an industry with only a few producers tending towards price dictatorship)/monopolies
   - More bankruptcies of small and medium-sized enterprises

   Typical problems have arisen due to:
   - cultural differences in cross-border mergers
   - information technology incompatibility
   - management conflict

   Some companies have been forced to abandon merger plans or even to demerge when they have become the target of antitrust regulators/monopoly commissioners.

Role-play *257*

This is a preparation activity for writing the business report. The role-play can be done either as a face-to-face activity or as a phone call. If required students refer to Making Contact and Telephoning respectively.

258 –259 THE REPORT

Students are given some time to go through the report before giving a brief oral summary. They should also refer to the Reference Section (pp. 280–281).

260 – 263 Role-play

Students should use their creative potential here. Remember this is the basis for the next section on report writing.

263 Report writing

The report done by Christian can be used as a guideline. Samples of other reports can be located via an Internet search.

264 Vocabulary check

1. Purchase or takeover of a company. *acquisition*
2. Co-operation between two countries or organisations. *joint venture*
3. Relating to products that have a high prestige. *upmarket*
4. A company owned by a parent company. *subsidiary*
5. A large organisation consisting of a group of companies that manufacture or offer a wide variety of goods and services. *conglomerate*
6. To begin or *launch* a takeover bid.
7. Opposite of friendly takeover. *hostile takeover*
8. To identify. *pinpoint*
9. Being the only one of a particular type. *unique*
10. Another word for checking sth, e.g. a merger proposal. *investigating*

ADDITIONAL EXERCISE: PRESENTING INFORMATION

(Not in Student's Book)

This is a revision exercise that can be done before commencing the simulation.

Read the following extract of a report from the German IT company CPN and fill in the blanks using the words/phrases below. ▶ Note: There are **two** correct **possibilities** for each blank space between **(1)** – **(11)**.

In 1980, profits at CPN fell by £2.8m, a **(1)** _____/_____ of over 8% on the previous year's results. These bad results weren't welcomed by the shareholders and, as a result, share prices reached a **(2)** ______/________of 276p on the London Stock Exchange. Profits **(3)**________/_______ further in 1981 falling to a new low of £7.9m.
New management helped reverse the trend with sales and profits **(4)** ______/_______ slowly, resulting in a slight increase in dividend payments. Sales then increased **(5)** _______/________, but in 1997 there was a **(6)** _______/______ 24% **(7)** _______/_______ in net profit which meant that a massive dividend of 49p in the pound was paid out, an all-time **(8)** _______/________ for the company.
At the beginning of this year sales **(9)** ______/_______ at 2.6 million units. They then climbed significantly over the following months, reaching a(n) **(10)** __________/_________ 6.3m units in the month of August. Sales were then **(11)** _________/_________ for the rest of the year. The **(12)** ____________ number of units sold was 264,000 per month. The management, however, plan to **(13)** ________ all expectations by **(14)** ________ the average over the next three years to 528,000. Sales of their main competitor, Segal, **(15)** _________ 176,000 units, while Cocon **(16)** __________ 4% to 93,000.

1. fell	average	fall	drop
2. low	fluctuation	trough	fall
3. stabilised	decreased	exceeded	dropped
4. increasing	levelling off	peaking	rising
5. dramatically	gradually	steadily	suddenly
6. moderate	marked	dramatic	very sharp
7. increase	reduction	rise	decline
8. height	summit	high	record
9. bottomed out	stood	were	averaged
10. remarkable	minimum	extraordinary	peak
11. picked up	reduced	constant	stable
12. middle	medium	average	general
13. exceed	execute	defeat	frustrate
14. reducing	doubling	trebling	stabilising
15. fell down	fell to	fell by	fell into
16. fell to	fell by	fell into	fell down

Key:

(1) fall/drop
(2) low/trough
(3) decreased/dropped
(4) increasing/rising
(5) gradually/steadily
(6) dramatic/very sharp
(7) increase/rise
(8) high/record
(9) were/stood
(10) remarkable/extraordinary
(11) constant/stable
(12) average
(13) exceed
(14) doubling
(15) fell to
(16) fell by

264 **Simulation**

This represents the final part of the simulation. If the groups still exists with the same membership, they should now give a more elaborate presentation focussing on the positive development and the potential of the company.

The teams should be prepared to make a SWOT analysis (see Unit 4, Marketing Plan) of their firms as this may be required by potential investors/merger partners.

If the old groups do not exist in their previous form, new teams can be formed that represent a (real or fictitious) company of their choice.

265 WHEN ALL IS SAID AND DONE

This part represents the epilogue where Hazel is reflecting on her life so far. Students are asked where they see Hazel's future.

266 POEM – DREAMS

The students read the poem. A nice way to finish the book/course is to ask them about their own hopes.

INTRODUCTION

It is up to the instructor to use the Grammar Section as he/she sees fit. For weaker students it may be advisable to do it as a module before starting the units.

As mentioned in the Student's Book this section contains only a short explanation of common grammar problem areas with accompanying exercises and should not be seen as a detailed review of grammar structures. Students who encounter difficulties should use a reference book for more intensive studies. Recommended reading: R. Murphy, *English Grammar in Use. New Edition.* Cambridge: CUP, 1994.

More advanced students may wish in any event to attempt False Friends & Other Problem Words and Prepositions. The A and B parts of the Gerund/Infinitive exercise can be used in conjunction with Unit 10 (Doing Business) while the C part can be used with the discussion in Unit 1 (p. 10).

REVIEW GRAMMAR SECTION

315 1. QUESTIONS

A) Direct Questions

1. Who did you place the order with?
2. Where was the International Trade Conference held?
3. Why were you concerned about the quality of your product?
4. Who is Mr Whitcomb going to visit?
5. How often/How many times would you have to travel abroad?
6. How many subsidiaries does the company have in Europe?
7. What did the board decide in their last meeting?
8. How long/How many years did Mrs Chocolate work in Madrid?
9. What do further investments depend on?
10. What was the CEO accused of?
11. How long/How many years have they been doing business with Morton & Morton?
12. Where does the complaint have to be sent to?/Where has the company to be sent to?
13. How much does a complete set of equipment cost?
14. Who told you to get in touch with Gibson's as soon as possible?
15. Who/Which company are you employed by?
16. How do they send their consignments?
17. What do P & C not sell?
18. Who are the accounts being checked by?
19. What haven't we done in order to build the new premises?
20. When did they send us a fax?

B) YES/NO Questions

1. Does this company provide investment advice?
2. Will a merger be announced to the press tomorrow?
3. Do these letters have to be signed by the CEO?/Must these letters be signed by the CEO?
4. Are the premises being refurbished by a Czech construction company?
5. Did the American President sound optimistic about the prospects for growth?
6. Does a typical production process usually take four days?

316 **C) Statement Questions (Question Tags)**

1. Mike, you know a great deal about marketing, don't you?
2. You haven't found the file, have you?
3. Rebecca, you confirmed the order, didn't you?
4. We can send the catalogues by mail, can't we?
5. We shouldn't interrupt the meeting, should we?
6. They'll let us know before the end of the week, won't they?
7. Mrs Aston hasn't heard that the firm has gone bankrupt, has she?
8. You believe they are too expensive, don't you?
9. This building suits our purposes, doesn't it?
10. You won't send an agent to China, will you?

2. TENSES

A) Use the verbs in brackets in the correct tense. Change the position of the adverb if necessary.

1. Simon Howard (work) has worked/has been working for our company since 1995.
2. We (study) have studied practically every unit in the book so far.
3. The postman (deliver) delivered the letters just a few minutes ago.
2. He (work) had worked as a bank clerk before he (go) went to London to study International Law.
5. Only two students in this group (never be) have never been to England.
6. Peter (already apply) has already applied twice for a place at a British university.
4. We (receive) received the fax at 7pm last night.
5. Before his retirement Mr Rider (work) (had) worked/had been working here for almost twenty years.
9. Paul (study) has been studying/has studied Business Administration for one year now.
10. I cannot go to the party as I (not finish) haven't finished my work yet.

B) Fill in the correct preposition/adverb.

1. The Chief Accountant has been working here for twelve years.
2. I met him five years ago at an international conference.
3. I haven't met him since we left university.
4. The Purchasing Manager will be away on business for a week.
5. During his absence Miss Sunshine will stand in for him.
6. Sales have fallen dramatically since the end of last year.
7. Would you mind waiting here until he comes?
8. Payment has been overdue for five weeks.
9. We did business with them for more than ten years and had no problems at all during that time.
10. We regret that they had to file for bankruptcy three days ago.

C) Choose the best alternative to complete the sentence. (The position of the adverb may change.) 317

1. We have had the new computer since April.
2. Do you know whether the consignment has arrived?
3. I wish I knew a solution.
4. She was on a business trip last week.
5. Peter had been writing/had written the report before he went abroad.
6. I can't meet you tomorrow morning. I am attending/am going to attend a product presentation.
7. Our customers will probably like the new product.
8. Computers work faster than human beings.
9. The secretary was still typing the report when I arrived.
10. We are pleased to inform you that we have almost completed production.
11. The MD generally arrives at his office at 9 am.
12. Many people believe that VW is Germany's best car manufacturer.
13. Sales figures may rise when they launch their new product.
14. I can't attend the meeting this afternoon. I am going to Leipzig to sign the contract with Martin & Co.

317 – 318 **D) Situations. Put the verbs in brackets into the correct tense. Pay attention to the position of the adverb.**

1. Peggy (be) has been a student of Business Administration at Dresden University of Technology since October last year. Before she (begin) began her studies, she (work) (had) worked/had been working as a waitress for six months. She (always be) has always been an ambitious and hard-working person. Peggy (already get in touch) has already got in touch with an Irish computer company as she (plan) plans/is planning to do her compulsory industrial placement in Ireland.

2. Sheila Comer is the Chief Accountant of our company. She (work) has been working for us since she (graduate) graduated from university 15 years ago.

3. Anne (look) looks happy. The boss (just tell) has just told her she (be promoted) has been promoted/is going to be promoted. That's the best news she (have) has had for months. She (celebrate) is going to celebrate/will celebrate tonight.

4. Mr Reynolds is not in his office. He (go) went out for lunch five minutes ago and (not be) won't be back before 2pm. But I think Mrs Murphy (also be able) will also be able to help you, as she (deal with) deals/is dealing with the same project.

4. John Smith is one of the most successful sales representatives we (ever have) have ever had. I (know) have known him for many years and (never hear) have never heard any complaints about him.

318 **3. PASSIVE VOICE**

A) Transform the following sentences into the passive voice. Leave out the subjects whenever possible.

1. The consignment is urgently needed.
2. The accounts have to be checked regularly.
3. The equipment will be delivered next week.
4. New staff have been recruited.
5. The new subsidiary in Belgium will be opened by our MD.
6. The damaged parts are expected to be returned./We are expected to return the damaged parts.
7. The contract which was signed last week has not been seen (by anybody).
8. A discount of ten per cent was promised./We were promised a discount of ten per cent for regular orders.
9. Redundancies have never been talked about by the management.
10. She is just being shown the new pilot plant./The new pilot plant is just being shown to her.
11. We hope we will be granted a credit./We hope a credit will be granted.
12. Have the necessary arrangements been made?
13. Was Sven given a bonus?
14. Some more details have to be dealt with before an agreement can be arrived at.
15. We have been asked to dispatch the goods without delay.
16. I was told when I applied for the job that I would have to travel a lot.

17. The goods were sent to their customers after they had been manufactured.
18. They would have met the target if more staff had been employed./The target would have been met if more staff had been employed.
19. The proposal form has to be completed by the person who wants insurance cover.
20. Vast sums are paid annually into insurance funds.
21. Please let us know if a customs declaration is required.
22. The World Bank was established at the Bretton Woods Conference in 1944.
23. The company's range of products is being expanded.
24. The new marketing strategy has to be talked about at our next meeting.
25. The new distribution system has been made use of since the beginning of January.

4. REPORTED SPEECH 319

A) Put the following statements into Reported Speech.

1. Peter told me that Peggy hadn't passed her degree examination.
2. She said that they had discussed the new marketing strategy at their meeting the day before/ the previous day.
3. He informed us that he would probably go to France next week/the following week to negotiate the new contract with their/our business partners there.
4. The production manager told the MD that there had/have been many complaints about the new vending machine.
5. The sales manager decided that we/he would offer them a 15 percent discount.
6. Anne Meadow warns that they/we won't manage to deliver on time.
7. The Sales Manager assured us that if we weren't satisfied with the goods we could return them.
8. Peggy says that she wants to inform her boss first.
9. The chief accountant complained that the cost couldn't be covered.
10. The GM said that he/she was only trying to do what he/she thought was best for the corporation.
11. Tom replied that they owed us/them a fortune.
12. The R&D Manager reminded us that we would/will have to hand in the proposal by the end of the week.
13. I have always said that our products have to be improved.
14. The commission stated that nothing had been done to solve the problem.

B) Reported/Indirect Questions

1. He asked when I/we would deliver the goods.
2. She wanted to know why they had cancelled the order.
3. He asked which product I/(s)he/they was/were talking about.
4. She asked him where the quotation forms are/were/if he could tell her where the quotation forms are/were.
5. He asked me if/our/my company is/was based in Singapore.
6. He asked if the goods would be delivered on time.
7. Tom asked if she had cashed the cheque the day before.
8. Rob Donovan asked me if I/we could lend them some money.

320 5. CONDITIONALS

A) Use the following phrases and make three conditional sentences.

1.
   If you order large quantities, the company will offer you a discount.
   If you ordered large quantities, the company would offer you a discount.
   If you had ordered large quantities, the company would have offered you a discount.
2.
   If you complete the form, you'll get a refund.
   If you completed the form, you'd get a refund.
   If you'd completed the form, you would have got a refund.
3.
   If you apply for the job, you'll get it.
   If you applied for the job, you'd get it.
   If you'd applied for the job, you would have got it.
4.
   If you confirm the order, they'll start with production immediately.
   If you confirmed the order, they'd start with production immediately.
   If you'd confirmed the order, they would have started with production immediately.
5.
   If our customers are not satisfied, we'll change the product.
   If our customers were not satisfied, we'd change the product.
   If our customers had not been satisfied, we would have changed the product.

B) Complete the following sentences.

1. If I were the Managing Director, I would ...
2. Unless we economise on raw material, we will ...
3. If the car industry expanded rapidly, it would ...
4. Unless you turn up well-prepared for a job interview, you won't ...
5. The company will have to cut jobs if it doesn't/can't, etc ...
6. If we knew the latest sales figures, we would/could/might etc ...
7. If they had employed more staff, they would have produced ...
8. We would have managed to deliver on time, if we had finished ...

320 – 322 6. GERUND/INFINITIVE

A) Gerund or infinitive? Put the verbs in brackets into the correct form.

1. Remember to update the client database.
2. I remember receiving many complaints from overseas customers when the new product was launched.
3. We like to test the instruments before despatch.
4. I like talking/to talk to ... customers from all over the world.
5. We are trying to establish a new system of distribution in France.
6. Last year we tried working/to work with two different suppliers which turned out to be a mistake.

7. We regret having sent you the wrong goods.
8. We regret to have to inform you that we are unable to meet the delivery schedule.
9. If you want to get the job, you need to apply as soon as possible.
10. This is a difficult problem which needs thinking/to be thought about very carefully.

B) Use the verbs in brackets in the correct form. 321
Letter I

Dear Ron

After our telephone call last week I managed to get hold of Ms George of Smith & Socks Ltd. She really seems to be interested in our product. I remember mentioning to you that Smith & Socks are one of the most successful small enterprises around, and that I am very interested in co-operating with them in the future.

On my way to London I stopped to visit our Belgian agent Pierre Hugo. He told me that he had stopped dealing with Hammersmith Inc., as they have been slow with payments over the last months. They seem to be experiencing serious liquidity problems. P. Hugo expects to receive news soon of a takeover or bankruptcy. As Hammersmith's have just placed a substantial order with us, we should withhold delivery at least for some days. I'll try to find out more about this matter and inform you as soon as possible.

Best wishes
Ken

Letter II

Dear Sir/Madam

Our firm specialises in manufacturing computer components for the export market. We are currently in the process of reviewing our insurance cover and would be interested in receiving a quotation from you.

Please refer to the enclosed information for calculating the above-mentioned price. Feel free to contact us if you wish to arrange a visit or if you have any questions regarding our firm.

We look forward to hearing from you at your earliest convenience.
Thanking you in advance.

Yours faithfully
Charles Christman

C) Open to student's own ideas.

322 7. ADJECTIVE/ADVERB

Complete the following sentences.

1. If you work hard, you will be promoted.
2. We need the goods urgently.
3. Your new idea sounds great.
4. We haven't received any orders from them lately.
5. The MD arrived late for the meeting.
6. The machine is surprisingly simple to operate.
7. The job was done satisfactorily.
8. Our products are highly recommended.
9. I'm sure I could live happily without money.
10. The man became violent when he was asked to leave.
11. You look terrible. Are you all right?
12. There is no point in doing a job if you don't do it properly.
13. The restaurant was reasonably cheap.
14. Mary learns languages incredibly quickly.
15. Susan plays the piano well.
16. Do you feel nervous before exams?
17. I'd like to buy a car, but it's absolutely impossible for me at the moment.
18. Everything was very quiet. There was complete silence.
19. The profit is not particularly good.
20. There are very strong economic arguments for reducing investments.
21. In the long term reducing R&D spending is not economical.
22. He spoke enthusiastically about the new products.
23. The information given was really relevant.
24. Although the equipment is old it works relatively reliably.

Use comparatives/superlatives with the following.

25. The longer I waited for my interview the quieter I became.
26. The new machine is less reliable than the old one.
27. Why does he always phone me at the worst possible moment?
28. Petrol is twice as expensive as it was a few years ago.
29. The latest figures seem more/less promising than expected.
30. This was the most intensively used material we have ever had.

323 8. PREPOSITIONS

Insert the correct preposition.

1. There is a great demand for their products in France.
2. The company is spending too much money on non-productive items.
3. He received a cheque for $1000.
4. She is an expert in developing tailor-made software.
5. Mrs Tiger welcomed the guest on behalf of the Board of Directors.

6. The new subsidiary specialises in producing spare parts.
7. They were unable to deliver on time as some parts were not in stock, i.e. they were out of stock.
8. Our new products are sold at a higher price.
9. The new machines were shown at the Leipzig Trade Fair last year.
10. The company deals in computer software.
11. He apologised for being late.
12. Which is the next item on the agenda?
13. It is difficult to predict any results at this stage of the negotiations.
14. The goods delivered do not comply with the order.
15. Their partners sell the goods at their own risk.
16. This service is offered free of charge.
17. All arrangements are subject to confirmation.
18. Sven Halliday is responsible to the MD (i.e. he reports to him).
19. The company has been short of funds for months.
20. We are most grateful to him for his support.
21. They sent them a cheque in payment for the goods.
22. They have placed an order for 150 monitors.
23. We hope to sell the goods at a profit and not at a loss.
24. Were the goods sent by air or sea?
25. They sent us a fax in reply to our letter.
26. We never sell on credit.
27. We need the part by 1 April at the latest.
28. I have an appointment with the Personnel Manager on 30 June at 10am.
29. They are regular customers and have placed orders with us for many years.
30. Would you please send us some information about/on your new product.
31. We are disappointed with/by the service.
32. Workers earn $500 on average.
33. We will send you a quotation on request.
34. The bill has to be settled within 2 weeks.
35. Mr Moon is employed by our company in Paris.
36. John has a house in the suburbs.
37. Follow the signs to get to Dublin.
38. Turn right at the next traffic lights, the factory is opposite/near/in front of/behind/etc the school.
39. If you drive down the N16 you will come out on a main road.

9. FALSE FRIENDS AND OTHER PROBLEM WORDS

324 – 326

A. Fill in the correct word in the correct form.

1. I have an urgent appointment with the bank tomorrow. Afterwards I have a date with my boy-friend.
2. The employees expect a 5% pay rise (BE)/raise (AE). The reality is that the firm will have to raise a credit to cover this.

3. What was the cause of delay in production yesterday? I will need a satisfactory reason.
4. As we all know, the bank manager lends and the poor customer borrows.
5. Let's be realistic. John is very sensitive and it wasn't very sensible to upset him.
6. The canteen is near the main plant and the parking lot is nearby.
7. According to the leading economist in the country the economic situation is not getting any better so people will need to be more economical.
8. Americans refer to the Personnel Department as Human Resources. I have a personal problem at the moment.
9. The losses at the firm are having a negative effect (noun) on the staff in that it is going to affect (verb) their work.
10. The principal objective is to increase sales, don't let a personal principle interfere with this.
11. The interesting thing about the company is that their manager is really interested in the welfare of his staff.
12. I can't spare any money for a holiday as I have to save for a new car.
13. The current situation is not too optimistic, the actual number of people unemployed is now 4 million.
14. I am working so hard these days that there is hardly any time to relax.
15. I'm not going to the restaurant where I'll have to sit beside some boring managers and besides, I have a bad cold.
16. We are now entering passport control where there will be a passport check. Those whose passports prove not to be in order will not gain entry.
17. I checked the date on the calendar on the wall, now I'm going to write it into my diary (BE)/ calendar (AE).
18. John eventually passed his exams but it will be Thursday or possibly Friday before he gets a certificate.
19. The police investigation concluded that the criminal gang had made a substantial investment in Al Capone Inc.
20. He's a good manager with clear morals, perhaps that's why staff morale is so high.
21. He's a really nice guy so I was very sympathetic when I heard that he had lost his job.
22. I have a really good job but there is often too much work.
23. I am going on a one-year journey through South America before I start my career. The voyage there by ship will last two weeks. My father travels a lot, too, but he only goes on short business trips.

▶ Note: *Trip, journey* and *travel* are sometimes confused.
Trip and *journey* are countable nouns, *travel* is uncountable, used mainly as a verb or in the expression *Travel broadens the mind. Trip* suggests business/pleasure or is found in expressions like: day trip, round trip (AE), overnight trip. A *journey* can also be business/ pleasure but the focus is on the fact of travelling rather than the reason, e.g. *The journey takes two hours.*

24. It's easier to fly to London. The flight only takes two hours, leaving some time for a sightseeing trip to take in the most important sights.
25. It's not my fault that a mistake was made. Perhaps it was a computer error.
26. She was very lucky to find a job as unemployment is so high, but she isn't too happy with the low salary and long hours.
27. 'Have you all finished your reports yet as the marketing manager is ready to start going through them.

28. 'Speaker A: Imagine we were all millionaires and owned successful businesses! You have no idea of how happy I would be. Speaker B: What a great imagination you've got!
29. 'John's party was great fun but I thought it a bit funny of him to insult and tell such a lot of funny jokes about the management. He never came to work again and there is over $800K (K = kilo = thousand) missing from the company's account. John was last seen in South America.
30. Safety (physical) in a car is provided in part with a safety belt. Your car is protected from theft by a security (psychological) mechanism such as an alarm system.
31. I had to accept the small pay rise. Everyone did except John, who was very angry.
32. I would be really grateful if you could advise (verb) me on what to do. Michael's advice (noun) was totally useless.
33. We were all ready to start the conference. Most of the delegates were already present.
34. 1,2,3,4,5 are simple numbers. When they are manipulated, i.e. added, subtracted etc we get figures (BE)/numbers (AE).
35. I didn't recognise him at first, but a few minutes later I realised that he was the President of the company.
36. He is lying there on the sofa telling every lie under the sun. I'm sure he stole my wallet, which I had laid on the table.

▶ Note: One meaning of *lie* is to tell an untruth. *To lie* also means to be on a horizontal surface. (Not used with an object.) *To lay* means to put or place something on a horizontal surface. (Must have an object.)

37. I meet him regularly at social and business functions. He's really an outgoing and sociable kind of person.
38. I prefer the CNN channel because of its good news programme(s). The only other thing I like is *Friends*. It is a really good series consisting of about 150 episodes.
39. A refund is money given back, usually for faulty or unwanted goods after payment has been made. A discount is a reduction in the usual price of something before payment, while a rebate is given for the overpayment of rent, rates or tax.
40. The threat of redundancies was mentioned every week by management. The trade union leader felt that this was no way to treat the employees. After work he bought his kid an ice-cream as a treat.

326 **B. Here are some German words for which there are similar words in English. The meanings, however, are different. Please find the appropriate English word for the German word and vice versa.**

Devisen	=	foreign currency/exchange
Lohn	=	wages
Kurs	=	exchange rate (Wechselkurs); price (Aktien)
Kaution	=	deposit (Miete); security
Provision	=	commission
Unternehmer	=	entrepreneur
prüfen	=	to check
Konkurs	=	bankruptcy
Rente	=	pension
decken	=	to cover
Revision	=	audit

devise	=	sich ausdenken
loan	=	Darlehen
course	=	Verlauf, Kurs
caution	=	Vorsicht
provision	=	Bereitstellung, Bestimmung
undertaker	=	Bestatter
prove	=	beweisen
concourse	=	(Eingangs) Halle, Zusammentreffen
rent	=	Miete
deck	=	Deck; Laufwerk
revision	=	Wiederholung; Überarbeitung